Stand for Truth, Cry for Justice

God of Beauty, Truth, and Goodness

God of beauty, truth, and goodness,
Lord of wisdom yet unknown,
Grant us strength to match the vision
As we come before Your throne.

Run with faith and live with honour
Bearing witness in his call
As disciples, build the future
Until Christ is Lord of all.

Stand for truth and cry for justice,
Share with those who don't belong,
And remember as you serve them,
Sing for those who have no song.

Make a joyful celebration
God in Christ has conquered death!
If you really are a witness
Sing until you have no breath.

Sing a joyful alleluia,
Praising God in all you do,
And remember as you witness,
God is singing over you!

Wesley Forbis
© 2000 Carson-Newman University

For Carol, Ian and Julie and Eliza, and Doug.

Your love and support, patience, generosity and sacrifice enabled me to write these sermons and to be available for the ministry that inspired them.

Contents

SERMONS FOR THE CHURCH YEAR

– ADVENT –

– LATE ADVENT/CHRISTMAS –

– CHRISTMASTIDE –

– EPIPHANY –

– TRANSFIGURATION –

– LENT –

– PALM / PASSION SUNDAY –

– MAUNDY THURSDAY –

– GOOD FRIDAY –

– EASTER –

– EASTERTIDE –

– PENTECOST –

-TRINITY SUNDAY –

– ALL SAINTS SUNDAY –

– CHRIST THE KING –

OCCASIONS AND THEMES IN THE LIFE OF A CONGREGATION

– ABUNDANCE V. SCARCITY –

– BEAUTY –

– LEADERSHIP –

– GAY PRIDE –

– SUMMER –

– CONFIRMATION –

– WORLD COMMUNION –

– REFORMATION SUNDAY –

– STEWARDSHIP –

– ORDINATION SUNDAY –

Preface

It is a happy coincidence that the opportunity to publish this collection of sermons coincides with twenty years of serving as pastor of Westminster Presbyterian Church, Buffalo, NY. Happy because it gives me and the members of this great church a way to mark our years together. Anniversaries are often recognized with objects that symbolize the number of years together; perhaps it's not inappropriate to recognize twenty years of sharing the covenant of ministry with a book of sermons.

In a very real sense, this book belongs not just to me but to Westminster. For as I learned from my mentor David McFarlane long ago, sermons are conversations between the pastor and the people in the pews taken together as a Christian community. And my son the Latin student, who knew I was preparing this collection, took a break from his studies and called excitedly the other day from Chapel Hill to tell me that the root word of sermon comes from the Latin word "sermo" which means, conveniently, conversation.

But while a sermon is a conversation it is not just any conversation. The conversation between a pastor and a congregation is charged, held accountable to, and finally judged by the mission and ministry that that community is called to engage in. And so, in a very real way, preaching and sermons are not 'orations' or 'speeches' or 'lectures' or well-crafted essays compellingly read. They are real dialogues between real people who have in common life's highest priority—to do justice, love kindness and walk humbly with God. And since we are wondrous though flawed creatures our efforts to live faithful lives individually and collectively are always works in progress.

More specifically, because we are the hands and feet of Christ in the world, the measure of our ministry is the recognizable stamp or evidence of Christ in what we do. The compass that guides this work is the Bible, and discerning the extent to which we are going in the right direction or need a change of course as a Christian community or, for that matter, as city or nation is rightly the subject matter of the sermon. The Holy Spirit enables such discernment. You could say, therefore, the conversation between pastor and people is God-infused when it works. It is also worth noting that while these sermons have the specificity of time and place, they deal with everyday concerns common to most people. There will be, therefore, hopefully, value, relevance and even perhaps a few glimpses of inspiration for those who are not members of the Westminster community but who choose to listen in on these pastor/people conversations.

I say, 'when it works.' I will never forget the comment on a sermon I submitted in Mr. Muehl's homiletics class at Yale Divinity School. The text assigned for a hypothetical Thanksgiving sermon was the story of the grateful leper. I had done an impressive job, I thought, of analyzing the nine ungrateful lepers and the one who returned to thank Jesus. Mr. Muehl's note at the bottom of the last page of the sermon was, "If you ever psychologize the text again, may your tongue cleave to the roof of your mouth." It was a good lesson learned. The Bible is sufficient for the preacher's needs, nor is the preacher a psychotherapist or self-help counselor and should never forget that he or she is a preacher. So, it's fair to say preaching and sermons don't 'work' all the time. But hopefully, over the years, a preacher learns how to mine the Scripture, be open to the Spirit and articulate a message that speaks to the pulsing heart of a congregation. As I look back over these sermons I am humbled by the congregation that gathered faithfully every Sunday to listen to them. And I am humbled by the grace of God that has let me continue to give voice to the gospel without my tongue cleaving to the roof of my mouth.

This is also a good opportunity to acknowledge and thank those who played an important role in my development as a pastor and preacher. My journey began before I was cognizant of it as a journey per se listening to the 'talks' of our youth minister, Reid Carpenter, when I was in high school. His weekly message was the bearer of hope at a time when my life was in a tailspin after my parents' divorce and my mother's remarriage. Then there was the compelling preaching of my pastor in high school, Bill Barker, walking the chancel without notes, exegeting the text from the original Greek or Hebrew, breaking open its meaning, invariably prophetic, calling our affluent suburban church to serve the poor and work for justice. In college, I began considering the ministry as a possible vocation and was supported in my soul-searching by the college chaplain Bill Franklin and my pastor in New Concord, Ohio, Caroll Woods—men of deep integrity, exemplars of pastoral ministry and preaching who helped me begin to understand what 'losing your life to gain it' might mean for me. In divinity school, I had the good fortune to hear William Sloane Coffin at Battell Chapel most Sundays—truly one of the great preachers of our time. whose sermons stripped away all the excuses of lukewarm faith and left his listeners with the decision to embrace the joy and justice of the gospel. And Bill Muehl and Harry Adams, my teachers of homiletics—two elegant men who eschewed false piety and honored rigorous biblical scholarship, and whose passion was to prepare us to apply the text to the realities and challenges of modern life. A succession of Beecher Lecturers at Yale left indelible impressions: Gardner Taylor, Fred Buechner, and Barbara Brown Taylor. It was Tom Troeger at Chautauqua who dazzled me with his remarkable artistry, creativity and poetry in the pulpit. And

Buechner, more the novelist and essayist than preacher perhaps, but who with his slightly rumpled, patrician style could lapse into almost mystical descriptions of ordinary moments in life that wove the gospel into my own joys and sorrows. Dear friend Charlie Staples, half a generation older, introduced me to Theodore Parker Ferris, the great Trinity Church, Copley Square preacher whose sermons we would listen to on Charlie's Magnavox record player on late winter afternoons in Easton, PA, and then discuss Ferris' impeccable logic and capacity to shine the light of the gospel through everyday circumstances into life's shadows. William Willimon has been a stalwart influence and help with his *Pulpit Resource* coming out every three months. His 'aliens in a strange land' approach to the church in America fits my theological and biblical orientation. Sally Brown, a friend from our first years serving churches in the same presbytery, went on to a professorship in homiletics at Princeton Theological Seminary. Sally's clarion call that preaching ought to honor its ecclesiastical roots in the New Testament and serve the ministry of a congregation has always stayed with me.

The benefit of having been exposed to these preachers is that the bar was high. They are some of the finest preachers of our time; but the downside is that it took some time before I found my own voice and stopped trying to sound like them.

That transition began when I served in my first call with David McFarlane, who became my mentor, friend, and brother, and was head of staff at North Presbyterian Church, Williamsville, NY. David, a superb preacher, did not hesitate to give me feedback, tagging ways to improve my content and delivery nestled in a larger critique that affirmed my gifts and bolstered my confidence. His own shining example in the pulpit was a weekly seminar in preaching: prophetic, yet even-handed in a way that kept conservatives *and* liberals on their toes. David's earthy language embodied the fullness of his and the congregation's humanity. He took an almost rabbinical approach to sorting through the text, weighing possible perspectives, delighting the congregation as we waited in suspense for his interpretation of what the gospel was saying to us in that moment. Invariably, he named our secret idols, spoke to our deepest dreams and lifted us up with the life-giving possibilities of people in faithful covenant with their God.

God's grace led and allowed me to serve on the board of Auburn Seminary in New York City simultaneously with my tenure at Westminster. I was lucky to be a board member when Barbara Wheeler was in the last years of her presidency and was then succeeded by Katharine Henderson. Katharine has transformed what was already a unique and indispensable institution in the world of theological education. Yet by the new millennium Auburn, like the local and national church, was solidly cast in the outdated structures of post WWII, progressive religion. Her leadership is the answer to what the Presbyterian Church and the wider world of organized religion needs, not just to remain relevant, but to speak truth to and powerfully impact a nation and world that seems to have lost its way. It is no surprise that Katharine and Auburn's example and call for leadership and social justice are woven through these sermons. The opportunity to serve Auburn and Westminster—two institutions for whom Micah's admonition and Jesus' answer to the Pharisees' question about the greatest commandment are the bottom line and final measure of ministry—the opportunity to be associated with these friends and colleagues over these years makes me think, at this stage of my ministry, of Simeon and the gratitude he felt.

This is the backstory to my attempts to participate in life's most important conversation—the ongoing dialogue between a pastor and his people.

My deepest thanks to David Russell Tullock, who opened the door, and to Matt Marco, our virtuoso IT expert, administrative assistant and accomplished choral accompanist—truly a man for all seasons—who assembled and arranged the manuscript. Finally, profound thanks to Dr. Reed Taylor, English teacher and American Studies scholar, who painstakingly proofread the galley proof of this book and removed my mistakes, significantly improving the final product. Without support from these friends and colleagues, this project would never have seen the light of day.

Tom Yorty
Buffalo, NY
Epiphany 2018

Foreword

It is an honor to celebrate this important milestone as the Rev. Tom Yorty celebrates twenty years as pastor of Westminster Presbyterian Church in Buffalo, New York. Tom has also served faithfully for fourteen years on the Board of Directors of Auburn Seminary, now celebrating its 200th year, so the marking of time is on the hearts and minds of all of us as we remember where we have come from and gather strength for the journey ahead. This coincidence of celebration also highlights a partnership between congregation and seminary that has stood the test of time, since the founding of Westminster Church not far from Auburn's original location in Auburn, New York.

Few professions other than pastoral ministry offer the opportunity and challenge of having something consequential to say week after week to the same community. What a daunting task! Other than a few years in congregational ministry, I have not had to adhere to such a discipline. Perhaps therefore I have found this collection of sermons to be deeply moving for my own meditation, certainly in content but also as testimony to the extraordinary body of work that has been created by this preacher over many years. These sermons now in essay form have fed my spiritual hunger during these times as they undoubtedly will for other readers.

As someone whose vocation is the exploration of faith-rooted justice leadership, I have learned a lot about Tom Yorty's leadership through these sermons. He has been deeply faithful to one of the hallmarks of Presbyterianism: the value of a learned ministry. In a season when many preachers string entertaining stories together and call it a sermon, his are theologically probing and deep; they explore questions of our human identity as Christians and children of God living in an ever more complex world. They invite a more capacious understanding of the multifaceted nature of God, Jesus and the lively, playful, disruptive choreography of the Spirit. These sermons do not pander to laxity, but command our intellectual focus and attention and call forth the best we can bring as listeners, readers, learners and actors. Like the lost art of letter writing, these preachments redeem the lost art of carefully crafted, biblically engaged, theologically grounded offerings.

Even more than demonstrating intellectual prowess, these sermons reveal Tom's heart for ministry and for the Westminster congregation. Without being self-referential, Tom is alive as a human being who loves God with his heart and mind, who loves his family fiercely, who loves his neighbors and imagines how they would wish to be loved, and he commends to our care the ones who may be different whether of race, class or creed. Daringly prophetic, Tom takes on the most pressing public issues of our day without flinching: gun violence, LGBT equality, care for Mother Earth, racial justice, and the evangelical/progressive divide that mirrors the polarization within our national body politic.

Which brings me to the people of Westminster. Through these sermons I have intuited a lot about you. You have loved this minister in the ups and downs of a long-term relationship. In times of joy and times of challenge, faithfulness abides.

The good news is that you can read your pastor's sermons again in this book and hear "more light" from these words. The good news for Tom is the deep satisfaction of being faithful in proclaiming God's infinite grace and truth for such a time as this. The good news for the broader reading public is that you, like me, will find food to satisfy your deepest spiritual hungers in these fearful and wonderful times.

The Rev. Dr. Katharine Henderson
President, Auburn Seminary

Sermons for the Church Year

– Advent –

Real Time Good News
Mark 1:1-8

December 3, 2017

Happy Advent! We start the journey today to Bethlehem and into a new Christian year. Each year we follow in the biblical readings the life, death and resurrection of Jesus which take us into Spring; then the birth of the church on Pentecost and the work of the church through fall, ending with Christ the King Sunday in late November.

Our guide in this journey with Jesus this year will be the Gospel of Mark. I used to think of Mark as a partial, watered-down gospel. Famous for his brevity, Mark lacks the sophistication and architecture of Matthew, the thrilling social justice of Luke and the soaring, gravity-defying Jesus of John.

Mark is the earliest account of Jesus' life. The other writers use Mark to frame their stories. Mark is the first to call his biography/history/sermon a "gospel". He invents the literary form. The ancient world loved stories of heroic characters, but Mark gives us more than that; he announces, as do the other gospels in their own signature ways, the start of an unprecedented era in human history.

But since my high school days when I started reading the bible and thought of Mark as a lightweight, what I've come to realize about him is how profound he is. It is easy to miss this quality because his sentences are like a reporter's notes—staccato phrases, glimpses of something Jesus said or did given in shorthand as if to minimize the record-keeping and stay focused on what Jesus might say or do next. What makes Mark so compelling is how his blunt description brings you so close to the action; and not just the action but the feeling—unfiltered, unvarnished, unlike the other gospels coiffed and primped for their audiences. If you read this gospel closely enough the text nearly breathes; if you listen carefully enough you might hear Jesus breathing.

For example, the very first sentence: "The beginning of the good news of Jesus Christ, the Son of God." No one had ever put those two things together–the good news of Jesus Christ and Son of God. The claim that the Creator of Everything came to us in an historical person was unheard of.

That this event qualified as good news in a world bludgeoned with bad news is what makes this a new era of history—the sentence shimmers with hope and possibility.

But Mark's gospel is no literary self-help pill or blueprint for salvation. He is comfortable with the ambiguity, contradiction, and mystery of human experience. The result is that we get more questions than answers. For example, the famous Messianic Secret presenting a messiah who shunned awareness of who he was in a world desperate for a savior. Why keep it under wraps? Why not shout it from the rooftops? Or most strange of all, the conclusion of this gospel at the empty tomb when Mark says the disciples simply ran in fear. Period. End of story. Really? A finale of fear for a literary account titled "Good News"? A later scribe adds a happy ending, but most scholars agree the authentic conclusion is the one with his followers running in terror. Mark leaves the reader with much to ponder.

His genius is to see that in the man Jesus is the beginning of a new era of history. History, to the Greeks, was primarily 'chronos' the endless ticking of the clock. But for Mark, history, time itself, is invaded by God through the man Jesus of Nazareth. The word for this in the Greek, meaning the 'fullness' or 'rightness' of time is "kairos". Time is both chronos and kairos. Mark is a theological Einstein—he sees the multi-dimensions of time embodied in the god/man Jesus and time bending through history to the opening of a new era of human existence and possibility called the Kingdom of God.

It is fitting that Mark has John the Baptist inform us of this turning, transcendent moment of history, this coming of hope into the world. Perhaps you remember from your art history class Matthias Grunewald's famous Isenheim Altarpiece—a triptych whose center painting is the scene of the crucifixion in excruciating detail. As the flayed, tortured, dead body of Christ hangs limp from the cross, on his right is Mary, the mother of Christ, and on his left Grunewald inserts John the Baptist in his roughhewn wilderness garb holding an open bible and pointing a long bony finger toward Christ on the cross. This is it, this is the opening of the new era; the pulling back of the veil of time and the natural world to reveal the heart of God giving himself in humiliating, ignominious death for a flawed, rebellious human creation. Who better than a near madman—the Baptizer—says Mark, and the artist Grunewald, to see the true meaning of such a scandal and travesty?

Here at the start of Advent, Mark's staccato strokes sketch the opening scene for his gospel: "John the baptizer appeared in the wilderness, proclaiming a baptism of repentance for the forgiveness of sins. And people from the *whole* Judean countryside and *all the people* of Jerusalem were going out to him, and were baptized by him in the river Jordan, confessing their sins." This is no mere political movement. It is a collective catharsis, a regurgitation, a throwing off of their misdirected lives and failure to honor their covenant with Yahweh. The "whole countryside" and "all the people of Jerusalem" are there to confess their sin and seek a new beginning.

We might imagine a similar culture-wide catharsis in our time, given the gridlock, scandal and chaos in our national leadership, the anticipated cutting of the safety net and the worsening plight of the poor. We might imagine a sudden societal 'sick and tired of being sick and tired' moment; a coming to our senses when we turn away from the greed and fighting and open ourselves to confession and healing.

But John was just the forerunner. His message was: 'Wake up! Clean up! Sober up! I'm not fit to untie the thong of the sandal of the one who is coming, and you are not fit to lay eyes on him in your present condition.' They came out of the woodwork, so deep was their need for an honest, chastising word, for his river ritual to mark their turning away from their misery. Given those other moments of history when people cried out for a moral compass and scales of justice that could not be sold to the highest bidder, Mark's account is spot on.

And here's what Mark offers: "The beginning of the good news about Jesus Christ, God's son." Mark doesn't say, "This is an introduction into the philosophy taught by Jesus Christ," or "an elucidation of some of the basic principles of Jesus Christ." Mark says, "This is the good news of the arrival of Jesus Christ, God's Son." He never says, "Here are the best practices of the highest achieving leaders in the Roman Senate or Jewish Sanhedrin" or "put these tenets of psychological wisdom to work in your life" or "try these daily rituals to increase your serotonin and happiness." He says, "Good news! God is here! God is with us!"

We've had great books and great ideas before—from tablets of stone that grew into a holy book of reflection and commentary on the care of the soul and neighbor; to countless practices from praying five times a day to refraining from meat, caffeine and alcohol to seasons of fasting and random acts of kindness—all of them of the highest and best human intention and worthy as far as they go. But all the books and ideas and programs, as much as we have gained from them, have not countered the cudgel of darkness that meets us at the end of our best efforts to save ourselves and change the world.

And so, Mark and the Baptist and Matthias Grunewald point to the Christ. Jesus didn't just bring us beautiful words or great insights about God. Jesus,

25

Mark says, was none other than God. When asked by Thomas how to find his way out of the gauntlet of hopelessness in his life, Jesus says to Thomas, "I am the way, the truth and the life." What Thomas and we get is not another spiritual fitness program but Jesus himself–revealing his crucified hands and feet to reassure us he is not a figment of our imagination; or Jesus calling us to follow and learn from him, holding on to us when we debate who's the best and greatest, not turning us away when we push others out of the way. When we are disloyal, he remains loyal; when we rebel, he is faithful; when we exclude, he includes.

This is real time good news. Not virtual good news. Or good news at the end of thirty days. Or quid pro quo good news. It is good news for free, for the taking, or not; good news without the hard sell (though some, selling something else, try hard to look like they're selling Jesus). This is good news without imposition, gimmicks, tricks or money back guarantees. We're way beyond stoic self-reliance or white flag resignation–either of which will provide respectful enough intellectual homes. But they are, in the end, tiny dwellings–like those popular pop-up campers.

The beauty and mystery of it is that Jesus Christ is good news, God's Son with us; so that life isn't circumscribed by the limits of our good will but open-ended with God's presence and a love that knows us better than we know our selves. This is the one who is coming and it's time to get ready to meet him. And the best way to do that is to put your faith in him with some circumstance you are facing. Not like a proctor giving a test but like one of John's repentant sinners, recognizing you've failed to live up to the best person buried somewhere deep within you. That's where you'll meet him. Amen.

Revelation and Faith
John 1:6-8, 18-28

December 10, 2017

It is a pleasure today in Advent to recognize twenty-three new members who became part of this church family in 2017. I want to talk about revelation and faith today. That's why any of us are here this morning–somewhere, sometime, someone revealed a truth to us. We each have a story about hearing and letting the revelation of that truth guide us into more abundant life; it's important to remember how we got here so that we can ensure that others will also find their way.

Consider John the Baptist in today's lesson. I read some parenting advice recently. It said, "Teach your kids the art of persuasion if you want them to be successful. Successful people are very good at persuading others. At its best, persuasion is the ability to effectively describe the benefits and logic of an idea to gain agreement." Teaching the art of persuasion may or may not be effective parenting advice, but persuasion is not what John the Baptist is doing today when he says, "I am the voice of one crying in the wilderness, 'Make straight the path of the Lord.' Among you stands one whom you do not know, the one who is coming after me; I am not worthy to untie the thong of his sandal." John is not trying to persuade anyone of anything; he is being deposed. This visit from the Pharisees is an official call; they are investigating rumors of the Messiah swirling among the people.

What John is doing in answer to the question, "Are you the Christ?" is testifying. His testimony is not based on something that he has dreamed up or concocted on his own. It is a truth that has been revealed to him. There's a difference between persuading and testifying. The persuader uses logic and the benefits of his point of view to gain acceptance of his argument. But the testifier is merely pointing to a fact, a truth that speaks for itself. He doesn't need to use the art of persuasion because the veracity of what it is he is pointing to is convincing.

Moral, ethical and religious truths are revealed truths. They are not personal claims or points of view that wouldn't exist if we didn't articulate them. We did not "come up" with the Ten Commandments. The Ten Commandments were revealed to Moses. And they were accepted by God's people because they are principles that surpass human invention; there is a transcendent, universal quality to "Thou shalt not kill or steal or covet." It feels right. It rings true.

I got a call from my son the other day. One of the things that disillusioned him when he was deployed in Afghanistan was the widespread abuse of children by tribal warlords. When he called there was a sense of relief in his voice; he said an investigation into the abuse of children by the Afghan military had been conducted. It was a great day for human rights he said. We didn't teach Douglas the abuse of children is wrong. He knew it was wrong when he saw it taking place.

Seeing John's testimony as revealed truth helps us to understand our role individually and as a congregation when we talk about what it is that attracts us to this place. There's a misconception in mainline Christianity that witnessing to our faith means persuading others to agree with our view of the Bible or God or Jesus. But the problem with seeing witnessing as persuading is that it turns our faith into an intellectual system rather than recognizing what it is and how it functions as a principled guide for living; a compass that points to true north when we are lost and seeking a higher path.

What drew us to this community, I would wager for most of us, was not an intellectual argument. Rather, what we hold on to, even cling to as we go into the world is a deep trust that to live a certain kind of life, to be open, kind and caring, for example, is better than to be closed, skeptical and miserly; and because we can't sustain that kind of life alone, we seek out a community where those truths are visible and real in the lives of its members who, though flawed, are committed to such principles. And here's the key: we associate this way of living with Jesus. We see in Jesus the embodiment, the human expression, of what the Creator of life or Higher Power or whatever name we give to the Holy Source of Life that is bigger than any of us and comes from beyond us intends for the human family.

Maybe you're thinking I have violated my own definition of revelation and crossed into the territory of persuasion and argument by referring to a divine source of life. But there is literally no way to argue such a proposition because there is no way, in the end, to prove it. Rather, such a statement is and can only be a conviction, an awareness, a reality that can't be argued but can be revealed. It lives outside the realm of persuasion and resides in the company of other revelatory declarations like: "she who loses her life will find it and he who seeks to gain his life will lose it" or "the root of all evil is the love of money."

It's not up to us to prove, defend or convince others about revealed truths; all we are asked to do is to be receptive to the witness of others and then to witness ourselves to the moral, ethical and religious truths that guide our living. And this relieves us of a great burden. The truth will take care of itself. The writer of those magnificent opening lines of John's Gospel, that parallel his telling of the story of Jesus with the Book of Genesis, indeed using the same language, "In the beginning...." to announce the creation of a new world—only this time a new world for God's people in second century Palestine—this writer tells us that the light that was coming into the world would conquer the darkness that enshrouds the human family.

And then he says, "there was a man sent from God, whose name was John. He came as a witness to testify to the light, so that all might believe through him." And the next words of that portion of John not included in today's reading: "God's Son was in the world.... but the world *did not know him*. He came to what was his own and *his own people did not accept him*. But to all who received him, who believed in his name, he gave power to become children of God."

We talk a lot about how important it is to be a 'welcoming congregation' but these lines from John's Gospel got me to rethinking that notion. Maybe the most important thing is not for us to be 'welcoming' so much as it is for us to be open to receiving and accepting the testimony, the revelation of the light that has come into the world through God's Son and for which we wait in this season of Advent. Clearly, it is not to be taken for granted that everyone will see, accept and receive the light. The Gospel says, "The world did not know him, his own people did not recognize him."

How is it that people don't recognize the light? That's a poignant question for our age and our blindness in the dark—with regard to the plight of the poor; or preyed upon and abused women; or immigrants seeking new homelands; or black Americans for whom the major indices of social, economic and physical wellbeing lag woefully behind those of white Americans, even white Americans with only a high school education compared with black Americans with four-year college degrees. How is it more people don't see the light?

Not unlike those in Palestine in Jesus' day we are distracted trying to keep up and survive; a culture of consumerism depletes our creative time, energy and resources; a drum beat of raising successful children dictates organizing and scheduling their lives to acquire all the right experiences and make all the right moves to get them into the right schools that will ensure their social status and economic success. Then you hear a voice crying in the wilderness like John the Baptist or David Brooks last Friday who quoted Jesus in his op-ed column: "What will it profit a man if he gains the whole world but loses his soul?" Brooks is not trying to persuade us of anything. He points to the light with a declarative statement framed as a rhetorical question that rings as true as it did when Jesus said it; especially in a time when a divided nation and ambitious politicians endanger our future as a democracy.

We're talking life and death. It's more important for us to receive testimony to the light of revealed truth than it is for us to sit here and say and think, if some stranger walks through the door, 'we'll show them we're decent and approachable and they can come back if they want to.' Don't get me wrong, welcoming is important, but it falls flat without our also being open to the light that transforms and makes us children of God. Being welcoming should be standard equipment for any church family; besides, by itself, it's a little passive; if all we do is send the signal to "come here, we'll welcome you, make you feel at home" and not follow with some effort to share from the treasure we have received, then what's the point?

Whoever it was who got us here risked rejection, risked coming off as imposing, risked being seen as a zealot or as naïve when they pointed to the light. Any of those things could silence us when we have opportunity to preach what we practice; to witness to the light. Good Presbyterians often demur when things get too personal. But, friends, we live in times that will not tolerate such deference and demurral where our children and the endangered climate are concerned.

I think of that long succession of saints who stepped from anonymity to point to the light: Paul and Silas testifying in prison so that the prison guard and his family were baptized; the great translator Tyndale burned at the stake for using common language for an English Bible so that even a plough boy could understand. I think of Luther saying to the authorities he had rebuked and who held his future in their hands, "Here I stand; I can do no other!" or Bonhoeffer in a Nazi camp befriending Nazi guards. Or Dorothy Day, advocate for the poor and homeless, Jane Addams and Ellen Gates Starr and their Hull House experiment in Chicago, or Rosa Louise McCauley Parks sitting down in the front of that bus in Montgomery, Alabama. All of them pointing to a higher truth, a light that enlightened their lives and gave them the power to become children of God.

For me, it was as long ago as the person who told me when I was 15 if I took the Bible seriously it would change my life; and as recently as a member of this congregation who is using his business to transform an east side neighborhood because, he said, "It's the right thing to do."

We have the extraordinary blessing of receiving twenty-three new members into the life of this congregation. I trust that you are here not only because when you came through the door someone welcomed you; but also, because through some program or person you recognized a deep moral or ethical truth that is valued here; or you were given deeper insight into Jesus at some defining moment in your life. All we can claim credit for is having the hutzpah and good sense to point to what is real and true and reliable for our daily living in this complex world. But the Source of light, Christ, gets credit for transforming this church from a comfortable congregation into a community of people not afraid to be seen as zealous or naïve or misinformed when it comes to pointing to the principles and values and truths that give us life.

How fitting that our choir is presenting Handel's *Messiah* today. Our text this morning is what inspired the great composer to write his masterpiece. Handel was not trying to persuade anyone of anything. He was pointing to and honoring, like the Baptist, the Messiah who was coming into the world. You hear music like that and there's nothing to debate. But there is a powerful truth that lifts you up, raises your spirits, feeds your longing for justice, just as it did King George of England, who, when he heard the Halleluiah Chorus for the first time, stood in homage to Christ.

Here's your assignment: preach what you practice; time is running out; darkness envelopes the world; there are people, still, who do not know or recognize him. Someone is waiting for you, someone distracted and trying simply to survive. Let your mind discern a face or a name. Then in some gesture or gift, with a phone call or letter or visit, point to the truth that enlightens your life. We live in dark times. We have light to share. Our job is to point to it. Christ will take care of the rest. Amen.

Patience When God is "Late"
Isaiah 35:1-10; James 5:7-10

December 15, 2013

You might be wondering about the cover of your bulletin—what does that van Gogh have to do with Christmas? Or perhaps you're curious why we're not singing Christmas carols today, (other than the Sunday School's wonderful retelling of the story). A local radio station has been playing Christmas music since November 1 for goodness sake.

There's an almost irresistible urge the closer we get, to say, sing and celebrate Merry Christmas before Christmas is here. What could possibly be wrong with that? Here's what's wrong with that: announcing, singing, saying Merry Christmas would deny us the marvelous, life-giving, transforming opportunity of waiting.

Surely, I'm kidding, you're thinking. An opportunity to wait; let me not take a rain check! We disdain waiting. Waiting is for people who don't know how to play the game, or don't have a seat in first class, or who don't have enough important things to do.

And yet, from the Promised Land to the Second Coming, the Bible extols waiting; both Testaments praise those who wait and wait patiently upon the Lord. What's up with waiting? Waiting for something is the first signal we get that we are not in charge. Waiting is a sign that other factors, other forces are at work. The farmer waits for the rain as James says today; the farmer doesn't control the weather, so the farmer must wait.

We wait for prayers to be answered because when we pray we are soliciting the help, the will, of a higher power; many of us pray for specific things to happen or not happen and we do so because we know that controlling such events is beyond our control. Prayer is born in desperate humility. We wait for our bodies to heal—well, actually in today's world we try to cut the waiting time with pills and surgery. I'm not saying pills and surgery aren't needed remedies, but we've bought into a health care mythology that thinks doctors can wave the magic wand of science and circumvent the natural, normal, often slow process our bodies require to heal.

The community to whom James writes his letter is tired of waiting for the return of Jesus. They've been told he will come again in power and glory.

They're persecuted, suffering people because they're followers of Jesus. They're ready for some power and glory on their side of the equation. Where is Jesus? What's keeping his return? Surely, he's late!

James wrote his letter a generation later than Paul's letter to the Romans. Paul talks about watching for cosmic signs that the end is near and Jesus' return at hand; but James uses the analogy of a farmer who waits for the rain cycle in Palestine to grow crops. James' generation is beginning to figure out what it takes to live each day waiting for the God of history to redeem creation, not knowing when or how God's intervention and justice will occur, which is our problem. Somehow James must find a way to go on living when Jesus' Second Coming is not as imminent or perhaps literal as previously thought; in fact, when it may not even happen in his lifetime. So, James invokes the prophets and Job as exemplars of what long-term waiting looks like.

I say waiting is the first signal we get in a relationship, in a career, or in our personal health that we are not in complete control. But waiting is also a spiritual practice which changes us: reorders priorities; deepens understanding; heightens awareness and widens tolerance; indeed, waiting transforms us.

One of the great Christian mystics of the 20th century, Simone Weil, said about relief from suffering that while God does not always take away suffering, God always gives us something redemptive to do with our suffering. "The extreme greatness of Christianity," she said, "lies in the fact that it does not seek a supernatural remedy for suffering but a supernatural use for it. Seeking pleasure," she continued, "is the search for an artificial paradise. But the contemplation of our limitations and our misery [in patient waiting] raises us up to a higher plane."

Another great religious mind, not a mystic, but a hard-boiled realist, C.S. Lewis, also referred to the transforming power of waiting, "A rational faith can fall to pieces when it is confronted with suffering as a personal reality, rather than as a theoretical quandary." After Lewis lost his wife, he realized he'd engaged life merely on the surface, whereas now his grief and lonely waiting for God thrust him to new depths. During his desperate waiting he wrote, "Where is God? Go to him when your need is desperate, when all other help is vain, and what do you find? A door slammed in your face, the sound of bolting and double-bolting on the inside. After that, silence." [i]

What the wisdom of those who've journeyed before us suggests is that there is no way to short-circuit, remove or avoid waiting, but these voices also testify to the unshakable trust that in our waiting we reach and dwell in new levels of personal healing and growth.

If waiting is merely descriptive of a passive state of 'going without,' patience, which James urges today, is a conscious choice. It conveys waiting without complaint, like those South American miners trapped for thirty-nine days last year; it conveys a steady enduring of circumstances like many of the families represented here today during the Great Depression. Patience also conveys a fortitude that relies upon courage like that of explorers Francis Drake, Lewis and Clark, and Neil Armstrong; and patient waiting relies on forbearance that evokes restraint from retaliation like Gandhi, King, and Mandela. Indeed, waiting with patience is what great lives, great communities and great civilizations are built upon.

When in today's lesson Isaiah speaks to the Israelites, then held in bondage in Babylon after the destruction of their homeland and temple, first he acknowledges the privileged class's bankrupt faith and their slide into corruption resulting in oppression of the poor. Yet, at last, he counsels faith in God who will not abandon them but restore their former glory after their suffering. In one of the most lyrical and comforting portrayals of God's restoration and recovery of his people Isaiah, the poet, describes a once drought-cracked desert in bloom. It is not a vision intended to be taken physically literally but spiritually literally. Whatever the spiritual equivalent is to a blooming desert, Isaiah says, will be true for God's people who wait with patience in their dark suffering.

The wilderness and the dry land shall be glad, Isaiah says, the desert shall rejoice and blossom. The majesty of God shall strengthen weak hands and make firm feeble knees and say to those who are of fearful heart, "Be Strong!" The eyes of the blind shall be opened, the ears of the deaf unstopped, the lame shall leap like a deer, the tongue of the speechless sing for joy. Waters shall break forth in the wilderness and streams in desert; a highway shall be there, in the desert, and it shall be called the Holy Way for it shall be for God's people. No lion or ravenous beast shall come upon it; and the ransomed of the Lord shall return home to Zion with singing and everlasting joy; they shall obtain joy and gladness; sorrow and sighing shall flee away.

It's a glorious vision and promise—not just human creation but all the created order will come to a day of complete healing and restoration. From the nearly irrevocably damaged bayou life in Louisiana and Mississippi to the hunted elephants of Kenya, this is the trust and hope preached from Genesis to Revelation in poetry, law, and history from one generation to the next and most supremely in the story of the birth of the Christ child, then illustrated in his teaching, preaching, healing and final confrontation and overcoming of the powers of darkness.

That's the bigger history and movement and goal of which we are a part when we practice waiting with patience for the arrival of Christmas and allow that path of "living without" to reshape and remake us.

Perhaps you saw some of the reporting yesterday on the one-year anniversary of the Newtown tragedy. The people of Newtown know what to us would seem unimaginable waiting in suffering. Yet from many of the stories it appears that, despite the long, slow road ahead, some have chosen to wait with endurance, courage and restraint, in other words with patience, while gun legislation lags and their community continues to pick up the pieces. Retired businessman John Ruffe in the bewildering aftermath of the tragedy wrote a poem that he carries with him and offers to anyone touched by that senseless loss of life. In its own quiet way, it evokes Isaiah's vision.

"Now's the time to swear and curse, about the world to think the worst," the poem reads. And it ends imagining the lost children whispering to the living, "Promise me this if you can/ That you will feel the dew beneath your feet/ And watch the sun as it lifts its head and hope/ For better things."

To choose to patiently wait for Christmas and the celebration of Christ's birth, which come in God's good time, sets us on a path that changes us. Great people, great communities, great civilizations are shaped and built in patient waiting.

The promise of Advent for those who wait with patience is, like a drought-ravaged desert or farmer who plants crops, that when the rains come the earth shall rejoice, enmity cease, and all manner of life shall be well. Waiting has nothing to do with sidestepping the roadblocks, detours and disappointments, but learning to embrace them. Amen.

i. C.S. Lewis, *A Grief Observed*, (New York: HarperCollins, 1961).

– Late Advent/Christmas –

Joy When God Upsets Our Plans
Isaiah 7:10-16; Matthew 1:18-25

December 22, 2013

It is fitting we begin the Christian year getting ready for a birth. Jesus' story, our story begins in a cradle. "A little child shall lead them," says Isaiah. But I wonder if we don't journey through two childhoods in life: the first, our chronological childhood, and the wonder and awe associated with it; then, the childhood we re-enter as adults, a 'second naivete"[i] in the words of French philosopher Paul Ricoeur, which sounds strikingly similar to Jesus' "no one shall enter the kingdom of God except like a child."

There is often the detour of disappointment as we leave our first childhood and enter our coming-of-age years, reluctantly realizing the things we believed as children may not be true. There is also a stage of discovering "the big world" that has an unmistakable sense of adventure, yet can end in disappointment, loss, and despair. Poets and philosophers call this "the human condition."

But it is when life is dark, according to Ricouer, that we are poised to enter our second childhood; when we realize that though what we believed during our first childhood may not be literally true, in adult life we are standing at the threshold of a wondrous world of profound, meaningful truth.

Here's what I mean. A good friend was in New York last week. She attended the Christmas show at Radio City Music Hall that includes the Rockettes and many live animals in festive procession—including camels! She was enchanted. And while I suspect she was not evaluating the production on its historical accuracy, her imagination and heart were captured by the story of this birth in a rude stable over 2,000 years ago; a story that signaled a new beginning for the human race, that promised hope and peace for all the world.

My friend saw that Christmas production through the eyes of her second childhood. Its literal veracity is not what she was looking for or needed. What caught her attention was the power of this story about the birth of a peasant

36

baby to a young, virgin mother and the capacity of this tale to say something new and much needed for our war-torn, crisis-ridden world.

What I'm suggesting today is that we enter these final days of Advent and then two weeks of Christmas with the wonder and imagination of our second childhood. In fact, the stories this morning from Isaiah and Matthew nearly demand it for they are stories that only a child could believe—either a child by age or a child by heart. The details of these accounts would be too difficult for a rational adult to accept. When Isaiah makes his furious pronouncement to the cowering King Ahaz, the king is unwilling to stand up for Israel against the northern powers. And this is the choice we confront in every century: placing our security in the old military industrial complex or placing our security in Yahweh's care and protection.

Ahaz cannot bring himself to trust in the providence and protection of God, so Isaiah gives him a sign: a child shall be born and before the child is of the age of discernment Ahaz' kingdom will be left desolate because Ahaz refuses to take a stand with his and his people's God. Ahaz brings this judgment upon himself because his ultimate trust is in human power.

The story is paired with Matthew's account of the birth of Jesus. There is a satisfying resonance between Isaiah's "the young woman is with child and shall bear a son, and they shall name him "Immanuel" (which means "God with us") and Matthew's "she will bear a son and you are to name him Jesus, for he will save his people from their sins." These two accounts of infants saving God's people from imminent destruction are, from a rational point of view, laughable and ridiculous. Which is precisely why these visions and pronouncements are so powerful—they use new imagery woven in a new narrative with an astonishing plot to break open the old myth that tanks and drones and armies will save the day and secure the future.

This new story, the story of God's Spirit at work in vulnerable infants and people recommitted to bringing God's kingdom into being has been told by painters, playwrights, poets, and composers for centuries. If we say "Christmas is only for children" because we think this story of a virgin birth is a fairy tale, we deprive ourselves as adults of what inspired twenty centuries of art from primitive Celtic sculpture to medieval tapestries to the Dutch Masters' biblical portraits to Bach's and Britten's choral works to Eliot's and Audens' poetic inspiration–inspiration so great it literally drove the social justice and reform movements of the 19th and 20th centuries.

But a child of no standing who turns away and defeats the force of nations and the politics of death, how could this be? Can a 21st century audience–to say nothing of a 1st century audience or Isaiah's audience of the 6th century BCE—accept such a notion? We get a major clue watching Joseph. In today's story, when he learns his betrothed is with a child not of his seed, his response to a difficult decision is the nugget of the story.

Joseph's expectations of matrimony and married life in first century Palestine would have been well established with little room for deviation. We take for granted, I think, the freedom we have to re-invent ourselves in today's culture: to change political parties, careers, even religions not to mention wardrobes and hairstyles.

But in Joseph's time everything was spelled out: career, daily life, gender roles, obligations to the state, and the practice of religion. No doubt he had a stable, secure, and peaceful future in mind when he was presented with Mary, by a representative of her family, as a potential bride. To learn that she had been impregnated before their engagement would have been disconcerting to say the least. He'd made his commitment to her public, the wedding was planned, the invitations ordered, and then this disturbing news, embarrassing for him and potentially lethal for her. He would end the engagement, quietly.

Yet Matthew says it was a dream that changed his mind. That's not hard to accept. Dreams are credited, through history, with great moments of revelation and change. The boy Samuel dreams Eli is calling him; Joseph interprets the dreams of Pharaoh; the prophets dream of a holy mountain and peace in the land; Abraham Lincoln, quoting the Bible, said without vision the people perish; Martin Luther King, Jr.'s great speech for racial, class and ethnic harmony was a dream. So Joseph dreams not only that he will take Mary as his betrothed but also that her unborn child was to have a history-changing role to play.

Or perhaps it's Matthew in this story who dreams the dream for his leading character in today's episode if you prefer. The point is when Joseph's plans and expectations for a happy, traditional family were rudely interrupted *he did not retrench and rely on the dictates of the old value system. He dreamed a completely new story for God's people.*

When faced with an imminent threat to his future he chose to stand firm, something Isaiah urged Ahaz to do; it's called being faithful; being true to your heart when it looks for all the world that you and your heart may get crushed in the process. I wish our politicians had Joseph's courage of conviction.

Once we decide to stand firm we are freed to use our imagination to reorganize the world, re-vision the present order, re-shape the status quo. Exercising imagination is the first step we take into our second childhood. What we perceive as monolithic truths and givens in an oppressive world are sometimes nothing more than the flimsy myths a child's fantasy can routinely explode. Myths that have weight and power because we accept their premise— "this is the way it is."

The need for gun legislation, reform for city schools and our excessive incarceration laws for non-violent crimes are issues close to the heart of this congregation. You're probably tired of me singing the praises of the new Pope but he is changing one of the most entrenched systems on the planet— the church—with simple, disarming, transparent statements of integrity. He speaks with the honesty of a child. He's closed the gap between prelate and people. I'll bet he dreams regularly of the new church.

Walt Whitman comes immediately to mind: open to a wider definition of gender roles and sexual orientation; celebrating, reveling in the diversity of the burgeoning American people. Whitman would marvel at the diversity of families today in America—one arena where the old status quo and definitions of a family as 2.3 children, a dog, a stay-at-home mom and 25-year mortgage has been transformed.

Apropos of Joseph today and his non-traditional family a recent report says, "American families are more ethnically, racially, and religiously diverse than half a generation ago, than even half a year ago. In increasing numbers, blacks marry whites, atheists marry Baptists, men marry men and women, women, Democrats marry Republicans." {ii} We're re-imagining the family in America and I must believe God is thrilled.

The time to re-imagine with the eyes of second childhood is when we face setbacks, like Joseph today or that resident of Newtown, CT I mentioned last week who wrote a poem affirming life in the face of tragedy or our President who is sending a delegation of gay athletes to the Winter Olympics to represent him in a nation riddled with anti-gay bigotry.

Change the story, rewrite the script, tell the truth in some other voice or with some surprising and different symbol. Community organizers tell us we must learn how to tell the truth more effectively with stories woven around it, works of art made about it; it must be communicated in new ways. {iii} Embed the truth with dreams for justice and the desire for equality. This is what Jesus did with stories and parables that had shock value. He startled the rigid authorities and jaded people with truths they couldn't mistake.

Prescription for happiness: let go of your possessions that possess you and follow me. Remedy for guilt and despair: dare to approach a God whose love is like the indiscriminate love of a heart-sick father who sees his long-lost son coming home. The path to healing and wholeness: exercise your faith and it will make you well.

The Westminster Economic Development Initiative had its annual meeting last week. Talk about reorganizing the old story with a new narrative. Bonnie Smith, chairperson of the board, reminded the board of its core vision: "to strive for a vibrant, stable, inviting community by offering business and educational opportunities to Buffalo's West Side."

An old world bazaar and a new world food court owned and operated by African immigrants that would become the main attraction at the heart of the West Side; in a neighborhood the city has been trying to revive for a decade and a half; a business that would attract suburban dwellers to a part of the city visited from the outside previously only by those who were in the market for drugs. Who would have believed such a thing possible? Not rational city planners or corporate executives or venture capitalists.

It took a group of church folk who'd been at work in the neighborhood building homes and tutoring children alongside their West Side friends; they'd grown fond of the neighborhood, decided to stand firm and start fighting for its future. Without any professional titles or urban planning, marketing or small business expertise they launched into their dream for justice and equal opportunity. A handful of church people who had entered their second naivete, their second childhood, started re-writing the story, changing the old givens.

The old story that poverty loses, greed wins needs some re-writing. Like Joseph, we start to re-write the stories of our families and neighborhoods and nation when we face some brick wall of "that'll never work here" or "we've tried that before," and then let go of how "it's supposed to be" and consider that we just might be standing at the threshold of something new.

The Christ child did not bring about change for three decades; it took a lot of trial and error before WEDI began transforming the West Side. Maybe you're facing what seems some imminent threat or danger; the Gospel today, late in Advent, says let God's dream for you capture your imagination and open your eyes to hope and wonder, then do what needs to be done.

Westminster member UB professor and African expert Claude Welch witnessed decades of apartheid in South Africa. Last week, after Nelson

Mandela's death, he was quoted on South Africa's 1994 first democratic election: "Lines miles long of men and women, some with babies on their back, others leaning on canes, ready to vote for the first time in their lives—it was extraordinary and one of the most emotional experiences in my life."

Joy filled Claude Welch; joy filled Joseph; joy will fill you and me when we let go of the old expectations and structures of division and death and embrace God's new moment. How fitting we begin the Christian year preparing for the birth of a child! Amen.

i. Paul Ricoeur, *The Symbolism of Evil,* (Boston: Beacon Press, 1967) 351.

ii. Natalie Angier, "Families" *The New York Times,* Science Times D1, November 26, 2013.

iii. Isaac Luria, "Digital Organizing Training and Coaching for New York State Organizers." Luria refers to "ethical spectacles" in his strategy for digital organizing and quotes Stephen Duncombe who defines these as "a symbolic action that seeks to shift the political culture toward more progressive values… The truth does not reveal itself by being the truth. It must be told, and we need to learn how to tell the truth more effectively. It must have stories woven around it, works of art made about it; it must be communicated in new ways. It must be embedded in experience that connects with people's dreams and desires, that resonates with the symbols and myth they find meaningful."

– Christmastide –

Lights, Camera, Action
John 1:1-18

January 5, 2014

When God Rolls Up Her Sleeves: Lights, Camera, Action. Today's story is a creation story complete with "In the beginning…" and light that shone upon a dark world to bring life. Appropriate for this first Sunday of the New Year.

Martin Scorsese in an essay on film-making said that making a movie is like creating a universe. First, there is light; a light we see considering, a light we are enlightened by. Then there is movement; the desire to make moving images is over 30,000 years old, Scorsese says, as we see in the primitive cave drawings of stampeding bison from Chauvet, France. And then there are what James Stewart once called "pieces of time." Scorsese talks about his fascination as a child looking into the movie projector to see small, still images passing quickly over the lens projected onto the screen. [1]

Pieces of time put together with other pieces of time that depict movement lift out of the darkness of our existence what Scorsese calls the "third image" or meaning. When such work, when "film-language" names, reveals, gives expression to the beauty, the grandeur, what even seems the unfathomableness of human existence it is a work of art.

The story we have today, so visual in its imagery, is not only a creation story, it is a great work of art. Indeed, after hearing these eloquent, majestic opening lines of John's Gospel it doesn't take much to conclude that we live, by choice, much of the time, rather small lives. Perhaps we've become blind to the grandeur, the unfathomableness of the incarnation; we seem to take this event at the genesis of our faith for granted—we've heard and celebrated it so many times, sung sweet, familiar carols about it, have acculturated it into a winter festival. But sometimes what is most familiar is most strange.

This text written during a time of Christian persecution, when Jewish Christians were breaking away from their synagogues to practice what was by then regarded as a new religion—called the Way, after the teachings of the man Jesus—this text harkens back to the opening lines of the Torah, the first words of the Book of Genesis, "In the beginning."

Jewish Christians would have been familiar with those words. Miracle enough that God brought into being a physical creation out of nothing. John's account, he was saying to his Jewish audience, is a new creation story—in every way as grand, remarkable, and stunning as the one from Genesis. Not God creating something nearly unfathomable in its expansiveness—the universe. But God creating something nearly unfathomable in its smallness: God taking the form of a finite human being.

John says it was Logos that is responsible for this new creation story. Logos was a Greek term that came into use in about 500 BCE thanks to Greek philosopher Heraclitus who said, "For although all things come to pass in accordance with this Logos, humans seem as if they have no recognition of them." Heraclitus here refers to a similar blindness John refers to when he says the world did not accept Jesus, his own people did not receive him.

Logos referred to the "mind of God," to the creative force expressed as intelligibility, rationality, order, and harmony. When John says, "the Word was with God" he means that part of God that orders, gives meaning and purpose to life and creation. Like that part of a musician or athlete that is their gift and enables them to perform great feats of artistry, technique and expression.

It may have been the Essene community that imported the term "Logos" into the emerging Christian vocabulary. We know the Essenes had a profound influence on early Christian ideas and practice and John's community. The Essenes also used the term Logos to refer to the energy or life force responsible for everything that came into being as well as the direction and purpose of everything that had being.

If John was making a movie he might have begun with images of the universe and deep, dark space at the time of creation, much like the opening minutes of the Terrance Malik film "The Tree of Life", and then brought us into the present with images perhaps of cells dividing and sub-dividing and then images of the man Jesus mingling among villagers and the sick and suffering, unrecognized by all but a few.

What John is saying in his account is first that there is continuity—from the first moment of creation to the birth of the man Jesus—this Life Force is one and the same. And the second thing John is saying is that this unimaginably vast and mysterious power that moves and shapes and brings into being planets and stars and nebulae has become, wonder of wonders, so personal, tangible, and familiar as a living, breathing human being with a face and hands that touch and feet that take him to places of suffering and anguish.

43

That which brought the worlds into being now brings a man into being, but not just a man—here's the genius, the art, the masterpiece of it—a man in whom this creative, life-giving force dwells subjecting itself to the limitations of the flesh, this vale of tears afflicted by heat and cold and hunger and disease and love. It would be difficult to come up with an equally earth-shaking proposition. The great discoveries of science pale by comparison: that time bends as Einstein said or that we descended from bi-valve mollusks as Darwin proposed or that there is order to chaos as recent mathematicians say. And unlike the discoveries of science, which are descriptions of nature's mysteries and anomalies, the implication of the incarnation is that this was accomplished with purpose, with intention to communicate with us, to woo and win our hearts and our allegiance.

Yet, we've reduced the story of incarnation, the Christmas story, to a winter commercial success and a "home for the holidays" festive reunion with family and friends. This is all well and good. But next to what it represents and why it happened, our secular, nostalgic version is miniscule. So if there is a take away from this story today it is that we, you and I, have continuity with this unfathomable power that brought the worlds into being; and that to those who are open to and receive this Logos is given that very same power to become children of God. What we say and do is animated, given life by nothing less than the Word, Logos, the mind of God that created the very cosmos.

An outreach ministry into an economically deprived community; a choral masterwork summoning the community to the life-giving ecstasy of music; prayers for peace offered up daily, weekly for individuals, communities, the world; a newly ordained and installed elder or deacon—all of it a continuous expression of this all-encompassing, purpose-giving, life-creating Logos.

I say we live small much of the time. Somehow, we forget or discount this potential inherent in us, ready at our disposal—powerful children of God. When I think about it, when I see John's creation movie I conclude that there is nothing we couldn't accomplish if we accepted him, accepted our potential. The bible is filled with story after story of God's people empowered, performing amazing feats with limited, meager resources against David and Goliath odds.

We are facing remarkable challenges as a church, a society, a nation and a world. There is hardly a better time to be a congregation; to be God's powerful children; to be continuing the unfolding saga of bringing light into a dark and death-dealing world. We have the power that made the universe to enable us to use the filament of our lives, of this church to thrill and illuminate with God's light.

Light that reveals movement, tiny pieces of time–images of us praying, tutoring, singing, serving so that together we create Scorsese's third image– meaning, purpose and hope in a dark time; a name for the mystery; a face for the life force at work creating, constantly creating a new world. Amen.

i Martin Scorese, "The Persisting Vision: Reading the Language of Cinema," *The New York Review of Books*, August 15, 2015.

– Epiphany –

Company of Moths
Psalm 139: 1-6,13-18; John 1:43-51
January 15, 2012

Perhaps you remember the old preacher's quip, "the good news is we have enough money to run the church this year, the bad news is it's still in your pocket." When Jesus appeared first to Andrew, then Peter in the Gospel of John, and in today's story, to Philip, then Nathaniel he wasn't just asking for a pledge, he was asking for everything.

"Follow me," are the words he used. What he implied was 'stop what you're doing, come to the place where I am staying, follow me from there to the place I am going. Learn from me as we journey together. Help me recruit others.' What would cause a person to do that? Something irresistible would be my guess. Something that held great promise, something that solved the deep riddles of life, something that opened the way to life. Something like light.

You know how moths are attracted to the light. In summer, on our back porch when we turn the light on, moths flock to the light on the wall. There is a marvelous book of poems by Michael Palmer entitled *Company of Moths*. He portrays in his poems very human, very ordinary people getting brief glimpses of the light of life in their everyday lives. Maybe we're all moths seeking the light. Hungry, desperate for the true light; and when it appears, when we think we've found light, we flock to it with abandon.

That is the way this call from Jesus comes. It's not a negotiated contract, just the invitation to experience something profoundly life-giving; something like light in a dark world. You can hear it in their voices in this morning's story. First, John the Baptist when Jesus walks by. He says to two disciples standing next to him, "Look! Here is the Lamb of God!" And then Andrew to his brother Simon Peter, "We have found the Messiah!" Then later, Philip to Nathaniel, "We have found him about whom Moses in the law, and the prophets wrote, Jesus son of Joseph from Nazareth." And finally, Nathaniel after meeting Jesus, "Rabbi, you are the son of God! You are the King of Israel!"

If you didn't catch it in my inflection you can see it when you read the text—exclamation points after each encounter with Jesus. These people have found something extraordinary; something they've hungered and longed for; something or rather someone promising fulfillment, wholeness, and deep peace. They're no different than you and me. We're all a company of moths hungering, searching for light.

Like a woman a colleague tells about. At mid-life she walked away from an executive job and became director of a center to teach teenage moms how to care for their children. How did she make such a dramatic move? An older friend who knew her well kept telling her, "I know you, and I'd be surprised if you can stay fulfilled just making money. You are the sort of person who wants more."

Another person who'd known her most of her life said, "You've spent much of your life living the plans others had for you. How about the plans God has for you? What about those?" Those people who helped that woman sort through her priorities and direction at a crossroads moment in her life were like Philip in today's story—they themselves were bearers of the light. That's how God chooses to work among us.

God comes to us in the person of Jesus and doesn't just start casting light on everything and everyone; God reaches through Jesus, out to others who, in turn, reach out and help to spread the light. God does not work alone. It's not unlike all of us gathered here on Christmas Eve when we start spreading the light among one another at the end of the service. First the room is dark, with only the Christ Candle and Advent Wreath burning; but then as the Deacons take the light from the single candle and spread it out among you, the room slowly fills with this glorious, golden, glowing light. One person at a time, growing stronger with each person who lights their candle. That's how God works through Jesus to spread light in a dark world. Gathering up regular folks who've known triumph and tragedy, using them to be light to the world.

You are in for a treat this coming Lent. Two of our "Wednesdays in Lent" dinner speakers are local leaders—the new Senior Rabbi at Temple Beth Zion, Gary Pokras, and Keith Frome, the Head of the King Center Charter School. Of course, on this MLK holiday weekend, we celebrate one of the greatest bearers of God's light in modern times. His following the light led him from fighting against racism to fighting for peace in the era of the Vietnam War and finally to fighting for civil rights for all people, for which he was criticized by some of his own supporters.

Rabbi Pokras and Keith Frome will share with us how the light of God attracted them to their present vocations. In Rabbi Pokras' case, how he found his way from being a non-observant Jew headed for a career in classical guitar performance to the Rabbinate. And for Keith Frome, how he made the move from heading an elite private school to serving as head of a charter school in Buffalo's poorest neighborhood.

Both of these are stories of transformation. But what's happened, you might say, is just like the woman who left the high paying executive job: Rabbi Pokras and Keith Frome have been recreated. They are different people. They did not do it themselves. Something bigger than them beckoned them. The first chapter of John's Gospel cleverly parallels the story of creation in Genesis. That's what following the light does; it re-creates us.

A little closer to home, a high school classmate of mine, who has done well, recently shared with me that he has fulfilled one of the goals on his bucket list–to find and thank the person responsible for leading him to the light. My friend credits his early coming to faith as the reason for his good fortune and the attraction to his call as a husband, parent, business person and, today, a life devoted to serving two medical missions and a youth ministry. I don't mean to suggest that he's perfect. But his disarming humility and deep generosity is the result of God's light reshaping him over the years.

The photo he sent pictured the two of them, Ted, and our high school youth group leader, Reid Carpenter, raising a glass to me–for I was part of that company of moths in high school, searching for the light. And I still consider myself to be in the company of moths searching, seeking the light.

Even though we may find the light at some point, in some moment of our journey, neither we nor the light stands still. Rather, the light of God, the light of Christ keeps summoning us, beckoning you and me to acts of justice and generosity, to decisions of consequence for ourselves and our loved ones, for the communities and world in which we live. That's God's light spreading through creation, spreading through you and me to dispel the reign of darkness. So being in the light is an active, participatory commitment.

And sometimes, though the light beckons us, it passes us by while we choose to remain in darkness. We succumb to the unrelenting glitter of material success or to the grind of routine, to the inevitable ring of misfortune or bad news, to the disappointment and grief we face because we are human and driven by hope and aspiration, yet life seasons and matures us by unmet expectations.

I heard a story the other day about a well-known preacher I greatly admire. He admitted that he'd been in a funk of late and over coffee with a friend and fellow preacher found himself complaining about his congregation. How they're not committed, don't really listen to sermons, and are easily distracted. To which his friend said, "Let me show you something," and led this well-known preacher down the steps of the church into the church basement. There they stood before a washing machine and dryer going full tilt presided over by two women who were washing then folding clothes into neat bundles.

"What is this?" the famous preacher asked. "When you are homeless," his friend explained, "one of the most difficult things is to get your clothes cleaned. This is part of our ministry to the homeless who live in this neighborhood. These good people wash the clothes, tie them in bundles, and put a note on them that says: "'God loves you and we do too.'" Suddenly, the well-known preacher felt unworthy to be there in the presence of such undeniable fidelity. Blinding, warm, wonderful light flooded from that dark basement. It was like the first day of Creation as if he'd gotten to see a whole new world.

I suspect any of us could recount how, though we've seen God's light and helped spread it ourselves, we too can find ourselves living in darkness; worrying about ourselves or a loved one; self-absorbed, bitter over some disappointment; resentful over some slight or lack of appreciation. So, we are called to be bearers of light to others just as we let others bear the light of Christ to us. In other words, we are called to live in the light, to dwell in the light of life as much as possible and to follow the light wherever it leads. Then, one day, we are called again beyond the partial light of this world to the Very Light of Very Light as one of the great creeds says into the great company of heaven and the eternal presence of God.

When we baptize a child, we are spreading the light of God. We are saying to that child, as we said to Alexander James this morning, "Come and see" the Messiah, the son of God, the King of Israel. We are extending the invitation that was extended to us: "Come and live the life God is creating for you." Amen.

– Transfiguration –

Our Truest and Deepest Purpose
Matthew 17:1-9

March 2, 2014

There is a tension in worship as there is in so much of life; a yin/yang, a push/pull of two forces that are essential, yet if one were to dominate the result would be deadly dull if not just deadly. I am talking about worship on the one hand as a place we come to get our bearings, to find order, perspective, and direction in life. And this is a good thing. The familiar order of service, the beautiful stained glass that surrounds us and soars into the blue ceiling, the glorious sounds of the organ and choir. For many of us worship is one of the most reassuring, predictable, stable, settled hours of our week. And we re-enter the world having regrouped, reconsidered, recommitted to the path we feel called to journey.

But today's story from Matthew turns upside down this orderly dimension of worship; this predictable, familiar space and liturgy of prayers, hymns, readings, and lessons. When Jesus took his disciples up the mountain they did not know what to expect; and once there, they found themselves overwhelmed with an experience unlike any they'd had before. Moses and Elijah standing there, Jesus bathed in glorious light, a voice from heaven pronouncing Jesus as God's beloved son.

They didn't know what to do. So Peter, from the hip as usual, suggests building booths for everyone—*who knows* what he was thinking, maybe he wanted to stay atop the mountain so rapturous was this moment. You see, the Transfiguration was the opposite of that familiar, regrouping moment we look forward to each Sunday before facing another week. The experience raised more questions than it answered. What was it all about—the patriarchal leaders, the light, the voice, Jesus lifted up into the clouds?

Whatever it was, whatever it meant, the moment lends itself less to a three-point sermon than it does to an expression of awe and wonder—like seeing the aurora borealis or a whale leap offshore on its migratory path. The usual reach of the disciples' rational, analytical capacity was insufficient to interpret the moment. They had no way to break it down and define it. Yet it remained with them to the end of their days; in their darkest moments, they would summon its mystery and grandeur; against the wall of persecution, they would recall its power.

In other words, this was a profound, life altering, shaping moment they couldn't even put into words but simply gave themselves to. There's an old hymn by one of the great hymn writers and poets of all time, Charles Wesley. It's called, "Love Divine, All Love Excelling." The last phrase of the last verse crescendos with these words, "lost in wonder, love and praise." Wesley is telling us the goal of the spiritual life for those who follow Jesus is to be in that place, beyond time, beyond words. Not in control with a neatly scripted liturgy but lost, lost in wonder, love and praise of God–it is our truest and deepest purpose.

Unless our worship–whether here or wherever we stop to acknowledge God in the course of our daily lives–includes moments like the one on the mountain when we are lost to our rational, analytical selves to wonder, love and praise, we run the risk of remaining in a spiritual rut. The poles of "spirit" and "order" create a resilient tension between grounded familiarity and expectation and awe. It is a tension created as well by the worship leaders and the worshippers.

Such moments remind us that there is a creative power bigger than anyone and all of us together; that there are values and truths and wisdom that no one invented but that come from beyond our limited human capacities and perspectives. Scientists and artists report such experiences; perhaps Bach caught more glimpses of it than anyone.

My hunch is most of us have experienced moments of transfiguration. I'll never forget one colleague talking about watching the movie Gandhi in a packed movie theater. And at the end of the film when Gandhi's body was engulfed in flames on the funeral pyre the entire audience sat there, he said, in silence, transfixed; 'lost in wonder, love and praise' would be my guess for this remarkable leader who was such a herald of human dignity and fierce enemy of injustice and oppression.

It's hard to say when we will encounter such moments. Rather than producing them by an act of the will the best we can do is be open to them. We can move through our days with a kind of peripheral vision, keeping our inner eye on the ordinary and mundane as much as the unusual, for God's beauty and grandeur is everywhere. Mainly we get too distracted. The visual candy of advertisers and our entertainment culture distracts us; the noise of

51

24/7 media robs the silence where God's still small voice often speaks. But today's story says stay awake, keep your eyes open.

I remember our son emerging from his barracks after spending sixty-three days from the Carolina mountains to the Florida swamps in Ranger School. The late afternoon Georgia sun bathed his lithe, muscled body and deeply tanned face and arms. A big smile broke over his face when he saw us standing with the other families across the road on the other side of the chain-link fence that encircled the troop buildings. Without any words he came running and embraced his mother in the deep hollow of his chest.

It was a transfiguration moment because—as for Peter, James and John coming down the mountain with Jesus now entering the second half of his dangerous ministry—everything after that encounter with our son would be different. Yes, I worry about his deployment in Afghanistan but the radiance on his face that day conveyed something that is difficult to put into words; a depth of fulfillment and joy, a full measure of confidence and gratitude transfigured him and reassured me he had discovered some deep peace with life. I knew he would be spiritually safe wherever he went, whatever he faced. Words fail.

That's what Jesus' transfiguration signaled to his followers. From that moment on they knew following him meant the path of life—come what may; though the nation was occupied by a hostile army, though the religious authorities wielded oppressive power and control—not just following but being in his presence was the answer to their deepest longing. You never know when moments of transfiguration will overtake you. But they will. I suspect the more attuned we are to them the more they occur. We come to Sunday morning corporate worship not just for order and a take away sound bite of wisdom for the week; we come also for potentially disruptive, dislocating, mysterious encounters with the holy. We're here not just to think but to adore, not just to redouble our call for justice but to make room for wonder, love and praise.

So come to the table and then come after worship to our celebration of Ellie's thirty-six years of humble, selfless service to this church and our music ministry. It's a perfectly good day to get lost, to forget *yourself* and be open to the mystery and grandeur of God's presence everywhere. Amen.

– Lent –

The Importance of Boundaries: Saying No
Genesis 2:15-17, 3:1-7; Matthew 4:1-11

March 5, 2017

It is no accident that at the start of the Bible, after God has created man, woman and the Garden, the first thing we learn—before we learn about Cain and Abel or the flood or the Ten Commandments or anything else—is the importance of saying no. The biblical writer tells us at the very start of the human drama—like a flight attendant on an airplane before takeoff giving instructions to the passengers about oxygen masks, flotation devices, exits and what to do should the plane go down—the biblical writer tells Adam and Eve what to do to survive life. We are given the gift of human existence, and here in Genesis we have an operating manual for full and abundant living.

This story in the Garden, which we will come back to in a moment, parallels today's account from Matthew of Jesus at the threshold of his ministry. Before we know anything about Jesus—other than his annunciation, birth and baptism—we have this story about his encounter with Satan in the wilderness. One commentator says, "something about Jesus stirs evil into resistance"; what we are witnessing is the moral/spiritual equivalent of that law of physics that for every action there is an equal and opposite reaction. Matthew tells us the same dark forces that emerged in the serpent when God instructed the man and woman not to eat of the fruit of the tree of the knowledge of good and evil are also at work confronting Jesus before his ministry begins.

So before he calls his followers, discusses the kingdom of God, preaches, or performs any miracles, the first thing Jesus does is to say no; and not just once but three times. It is an odd way to introduce the Savior of the world. But it is also what happens in Genesis when the man and the woman make their debut. The ancient texts alert us to the inherent longing in this finite existence for "more"; a yearning that can shadow our days, our relationships, our lives, yet violate and distract us from our best selves.

This hunger, call it evil, confronts Adam at the start of his life; it stalks Jesus at the start of his ministry; but whereas Adam fails to say no as he was advised, Jesus rejects the tempter's suggestions for how to use his power to enhance his life. It's worth noting the tempter tries to disguise his nefarious plot to distract Jesus from his mission by recommending three laudable, commendable acts. The dark forces do not always come to us as invitations to do that which we know we should not do; sometimes, they are more subtle and sophisticated and come to us disguised as good deeds no one would object to. C.S. Lewis captures this deadly charm better than anyone in his *Screwtape Letters*.

Each of the good deeds—providing food for the hungry by turning stones to bread; demonstrating God's power by throwing himself off a tower to have God save him, proving God's existence; or having power over the entire world to do with as Jesus wanted if he submits to and worships Satan—each of these offers tempts Jesus to be free of God, rather than trusting in and relying on God every step of the way.

In the Genesis story, Satan wants to skew the order of roles and relationships established at the creation: humans to God, to one another, and to the natural world. And, in Matthew, Satan wants to drive a wedge between Jesus and God. If he can confuse humans and distract Jesus he can accomplish much for his dark mission. As the texts point out, the only thing standing between the man, the woman and the serpent, and between Jesus and the tempter is the little word "No." But "No" is a word we generally do not like to say or hear. You remember the story of the little girl who prayed for a bicycle for her birthday and when her birthday came and there was no bicycle, crestfallen, she said to her mother, "God doesn't answer prayer." To which her mother replied, "Yes, he does honey, sometimes he just says, No."

'No' is a boundary, a fence, a wall. 'No' stops the flow of things. 'Yes' is open country, a free pass, a green light. You could write a history of the universe from the point of view of yes and no; the big bang=yes; black holes=no; peace=yes; war=no; birth=yes; death=no. We can't have one without the other. If we didn't have light, we would not know the experience of darkness. If we didn't have 'no' we would not know what 'yes' means. Paradoxically, each *defines* the other. That's what binary opposites do, as the poet of Ecclesiastes reminds us: to mourn/to dance, for war/for peace, to be born/to die. Opposites give dimension and definition to life.

Like other ancient texts—from the Greek poets and philosophers to the Upanishads to the Koran—these stories sort out our understanding of human nature, our moral and ethical responsibilities and the nature of God. The writers use literary devices of the time, parable and myth, to convey profound truths. To judge these stories as simplistic or lacking scientific credibility would be like reducing the value of a masterpiece painting to the worth of the frame or a classic car to what you could get for the scrap metal. If joy and sorrow define the emotions, and work and play human activity, and light and dark physical energy then yes and no define freedom. Neither one by itself is freedom, but the interplay, the dialogue, the call and response, of yes and no depict, describe, define what freedom is.

The story from Genesis tells us we have choice, we are free. Some philosophers and scientists reject the idea of human freedom. The biblical story tells us not only that we are free but that there are consequences when we exercise our freedom for better or worse depending on our motives and principles. The stories today of 'no' are stories of our freedom. Adam and Eve get it wrong. Jesus gets it right. The epic narrative of God's people is the history of a people who experience God's grace even when they misuse their freedom. These stories are our introduction to Lent and to the power of our 'yes' and 'no.' Lent is about sorting out the voices of life from the counter-voices of death that haunt our lives.

Let's look more closely. In the Garden, Adam and Eve are warned of this 'other tree.'—all of the Garden and its fruit are for the man and woman to enjoy *except* the other tree. This other tree is dangerous because it disrupts the ordered way of the Garden. It seduces humankind out of its proper role and capacity in the Garden.

The fruit of this tree skews the self-perception of the man and woman. They begin to see themselves as God. This perspective inclines them to long for the things of God, it takes their innocence and unleashes their rapacious appetites. The serpent is identified in the story not by decisive action but by his 'craftiness'. He creates options for the humans outside the options God has given them. The serpent is a means through which the gift of life is forfeited by falsely perceiving reality. The woman and the man misconstrue their relation to God, to one another and to their place in the Garden. The account is not only an indictment of their inflated sense of self, what the Greeks called hubris, it is an invitation back to the single voice that speaks the truth of our future.

Jesus, however, immediately perceives the false paths the tempter suggests. The power to feed humankind is met with 'humans do not live by bread alone.' Satan raises the ante: "I will give you control of the kingdoms and their politics if you worship me." How timely this old story. We are witness, these days, to a satanic hold on our politics and politicians. It is the drug of power! What's of interest is that Satan casts political power in terms of worship. "I will give you all this power (to do good) if you bow down and worship me." Indeed, politics has become, some say, a functional equivalent for God. The state is the source of our security, demands our ultimate loyalty and gives us purpose. If you consider the wars we fight, casualties we sustain and resources we expend it would be hard to think of another cause or commitment that demands such allegiance.

What Jesus does at every turn, and Adam and Eve fail to do, is practice self-denial for the sake of preserving his allegiance to God. Lent used to be a time for the practice of self-denial. Giving up desserts and other simple pleasures was a metaphor for denying greater pleasures that, were we to indulge them, could take control of our lives. What if the Christian life is as much about what we choose to give up, and say no to, as it is about what we say yes to? Such a perspective might cause us to ask what we are not willing to do or say because we are followers of Jesus.

John Bogel, faithful Episcopalian, founder of the Vanguard funds, who lives a modest life like Warren Buffet when it comes to material things, quotes Kurt Vonnegut and says, "I have something most Americans don't have, I have enough." Gandhi, for an extreme example, died with only a bowl, his eye glasses and his robe. Such self-denial is a choice not to be enslaved by material things, but to be able to say yes with one's whole being to life-affirming goals and commitments. The doping of athletes to expand their capacity to super human levels is the modern equivalent of the apple from the forbidden tree. Yet, these athletes merely mirror the values and aspirations of our society to have it all.

Where does that leave us at this start of Lent? If today's stories cause us to begin to consider exercising our use of the word "no" that is a good thing. Another way to look at it is that saying "no" to some things enables us to say "yes" to a higher cause or truer self or physically and spiritually healthy life style.

Jesus' final week is the quintessential illustration. When the crowds extol him and Judas wants him to start a revolution to thwart the Roman occupiers, Jesus says, "no." In fact, that revolution would come just seventy years later and end in utter disaster for the Jewish people. When Pilate, in the praetorium, gives Jesus the opportunity to absolve himself, Jesus refuses to betray his cause or his allegiance to God. Only in the Garden of Gethsemane does he express the burden of his mission and ask for relief, but then he leaves that lonely place of prayer to rouse his lethargic disciples and undertake again the events that would lead to his execution and death. But, of course, the end of the story is not the cross but the empty tomb. Good Friday's 'no' enables Easter's 'yes.'

Saying 'no' in today's stories raises the question of how we exercise our freedom. More often than not humans make a mess of things. Our longing for more, like an addiction, can escalate to the point of destroying marriages, families, and careers and if not destroying then distorting, confusing and wasting our lives. We say when you've made a mess of things enough times or when you've really screwed things up you hit rock bottom and suddenly get honest with yourself and everyone else, including God. That's Psalm 32 the choir sang today.

You see your rationalizations as distortions of what is true, but your best self as honest, humble, and giving. You become more consistent in saying 'no' to the voices of death and 'yes' to the voices of life. The person you are called to be, your true self emerges in your relationships and goals in life. All of it can come crashing down with a few self-serving, self-inflated decisions, so you make it a point to say your prayers and stay close to that higher being or power that gave you your life back again after you crashed and burned the last time. And you make it a point to stay close to people who are on the same path, who talk the same language and who will hold you accountable and support your decision to say 'no' and responsibly exercise your freedom.

No one can do it alone. That's why this church family from knitting groups to the after-school tutors to Lenten dinner circles and all the other ways and places we gather to get to know and support one another and carry out God's mission, that's why this place and the people are so important. The stakes are nothing less than life and death. Before God's people entered the Promised Land and a new chapter of prosperity and abundance, Moses had a heart to heart talk with them. He concluded by saying, "Choose life so that you and your descendants may live." It was the idea of women and men who were free to make that choice that thrilled God in the first place. Amen.

The Importance of Questioning: Not Being Afraid to Ask

Genesis 12:1-4a; John 3:1-17

March 12, 2017

The thing that sets humans apart from other species is our ability to question. What sets us apart from each other is our willingness to use that gift. I am reading Irish novelist Colm Toibin's biography of the great American poet Elizabeth Bishop (Toibin is the author of *Brooklyn*–maybe you read the book or saw the movie). Elizabeth Bishop was born in Nova Scotia, and was separated from her mother at age five because of her mother's mental illness; her father died before that when she was very young. Bishop was raised by a grandparent, then moved as a teenager to Massachusetts to live with an aunt.

Elizabeth Bishop's poetry is considered exquisite in its restraint, its uncanny accuracy of small detail, its taking nothing for granted in examining the everyday world and objects around her–her writing is nothing if not a lifelong questioning of the natural world, of human relationships, and of the human experience–like her poem on losing things, from her mother's watch, to her nation of origin and its austere landscape, to her lover. Almost none of her poems provide what might be called "answers" to her deep questions. In fact, her questions are virtually the answers themselves. They shape her life and give direction.

Bishop fulfills Rainer Maria Rilke's famous advice to a young poet: "Be patient toward all that is unsolved in your heart and try to love the questions themselves like locked rooms and like books that are written in a foreign tongue. Do not now seek the answers, which cannot be given you because you would not be able to live them. The point is, to live everything. Live the questions now. Perhaps you will then, without noticing it, live along some distant day into the answer."

There's advice we can take to the bank! Not easy to adhere to or practice, but there is wisdom and truth in what Rilke writes to his young poet. Living and loving the questions may be even more relevant now than in 1934 when those words were written, for ours is an age that is impatient and wants immediate answers. What this has led to, of course, is a steady diet of "easy answers" to difficult questions from science to religion and the bible, from health care to politics.

Indeed, the new health care bill in Congress seeks to eliminate the painstaking questioning process that led to the current bill. Months of budget calculations, interviews with consumers, heads of corporations, economists and industry experts are being cut out to quickly pass into law a program for the health of our nation that is based on little more than speculation and economic self-interest.

But a democracy is based on questioning—debate and dialogue in legislative chambers and judicial courts. This is the high calling of elected officials and citizens—to keep our minds open long enough to engage the debate, consider proposed and alternative answers and arrive at the best solutions. A commitment to open, unbiased inquiry is lacking in the current Congress, where ideological conformity and allegiance are more valued.

The truth is we often struggle to live in the ambiguous world of not knowing, of not yet having an answer. Carol and I are fans of the television show *The Big Bang Theory*. It revolves around four millennial 'nerd/scientists'—the epitome of which is Dr. Sheldon Cooper who thinks he has all the answers to life—a premise that makes the show a spoof on our society's blind faith in wonky, techno/science. For Sheldon everything, even love, has a rational explanation like when he says to his female counterpart, "I have a genetic propensity for you and feel our mating would strengthen the gene pool of the race." Sheldon is the logical, final outcome of the Enlightenment—the idea that reason will open all doors, dispel all mystery and explain God.

Because he has all the answers to life Sheldon is the most laughable of the characters. His oversized brain has stunted his emotional growth. His hero is Star Trek's Dr. Spock; but he lacks even Spock's half human self-awareness. The girl next door, a struggling actress and waitress, is the most human of the show's characters. She speaks a different language than Sheldon; her conversation is laced with emotion and common sense, so he never seems to be able to understand her.

Of course, basing our lives on rational deduction alone does not lead to ultimate fulfillment and happiness. At some point it all comes crashing down. Sheldon's meltdowns reveal the unpredictable and inexplicable side of life—like the turn of events that led to Elizabeth Bishop's loss of both parents at an early age, then the loss of her homeland. Yet, that was the crucible in which her questioning set her on the path to becoming a great poet.

Or Nicodemus in today's reading. We know instantly something is up when this well-known scholar of the Bible and religious authority goes under the cover of night to seek out Jesus. Something provokes him to take this risk.

We don't know what it is. Maybe the loss of a loved one, some impasse in his relationship with his wife or as a parent with his child, or maybe his well-ordered, low risk, measured life suddenly felt hollow and bankrupt of purpose and meaning. We don't know, nor does it matter. This is what Howell Raines calls the moment when the black dog catches up to you.

Nicodemus opens the conversation with Jesus with a compliment. "Rabbi, we know that you are a teacher who has come from God, for no one could do these miraculous signs you do unless God is with him." Jesus reads Nicodemus' heart. The flattery falls flat. Jesus gets to the point and names both Nicodemus' problem and what he longs for: "I assure you, unless someone is born 'anothen', it is not possible to see God's kingdom." 'Anothen' in the Greek means either 'again/anew' or 'from above.' Nicodemus stumbles on the word. He asks Jesus how it is possible to literally be 'born again.' And here, like C.S. Lewis' four children in the *Narnia Chronicles* stepping into the wardrobe and entering the Kingdom of Narnia, we leave the world of the flesh and enter with Nicodemus in this dialogue with Jesus the world of the Spirit. This is the world of the Gospel of John, a world of juxtaposed opposites—light and dark, good and evil, spirit and flesh. Nicodemus' problem is that he lives entirely in the world of the flesh—a world where human existence proceeds solely on its own power, is organized according to its own norms and rewards, and therefore is immune to the renewing power of God.

The world of the flesh is blind to the world of the Spirit—not to the *idea* of the world of the Spirit which the world of the flesh discounts and rejects; but to an *authenticating experience in the world of the Spirit.* Jesus tells Nicodemus, "unless someone is born of water and the Spirit, it is not possible to see (verse 3) and to enter (verse 5) God's kingdom." There is plenty of room for religion in the world of the flesh—we have a gazillion PhD programs in biblical studies, comparative religion, religion and ethics, religion and psychology, theology, ecclesiastical history; and there are more than a gazillion books written on and about religion. It is interesting that we read the sacred texts less and less and commentaries on those texts and commentaries on the commentaries more and more. Often, these secondary sources are merely rehashed ideas of a previous generation. So with each new book on religion we are further away not only from the voice of the biblical author and community but also any personal authenticating religious experience—that is, any confrontation with God.

This is the world Nicodemus represents. Given his status as a Torah scholar he is an expert in Midrash—the voluminous, complicated commentary on the Torah. Midrash is the endless debate by the rabbis of every possible nuance, key word, and legal application of the sacred text. It is brilliant and fascinating; it requires a lifetime of arduous study; but by itself it is not a gateway to the world of the Spirit.

Ironically, this controlled, God-dissected religion in the world of the flesh often undercuts the goal of religion—to love God and serve our neighbor: the rich ruler who keeps the commandments but refuses to sell his possessions, give to the poor and follow Jesus; the priest and the Levite in the parable of the Good Samaritan who ignore the wounded traveler; the Pharisees who object to healing on the Sabbath. This is the very world Jesus comes to disrupt, break open and transform.

The world of the Spirit, on the other hand, is an entirely different world. It is a world where the "ruah" or 'breath' of God in the Hebrew, blows, not according to human will but God's will. Just as the wind of the Spirit blew over the face of the deep at creation and brought life into being, so the Spirit blows into our lives and brings about the new church, the new person, the new creation God intends. People who inhabit the world of the Spirit are open and vulnerable to the untamed wind of God. How does one get from the world of the flesh to the world of the Spirit? Not by human effort but only by God's grace. Jesus opens the door to the world of the Spirit for Nicodemus—but it is Nicodemus who must step over the threshold just as the children in the wardrobe do to get to Narnia.

It is not clear from today's story alone if Nicodemus takes that first step. But he finds himself, in his midnight interview with Jesus, in a new place. Not unlike Abraham who heard God's summons to go with his household to a new land. Nicodemus, like Abraham, is faced with the decision to trust the voice that summons him. Abraham did—six thousand years ago; or we would not be here today. Forget John Calvin or St. Augustine or the apostles or Jesus or the prophets or any of them. Abraham was the first to hear God's call to enter the world of the Spirit, to leave the comfortable and familiar for a new land. Nicodemus is where he is in the story today because he was willing to find Jesus and ask a few questions. In fact, he was willing to humble himself, to trust Jesus, even to look foolish—especially for someone of his status and authority asking Jesus how to be born anew.

Which is where we began—we are the species that asks questions, and what sets us apart from one another is our willingness to use that gift. It is an art and discipline—Socrates based his methodology for awakening the minds of his students on a system of asking questions. No one needs to awaken the mind of a child; children are naturally intellectually curious. What looks like their play, said Fred Rogers of *Mr. Rogers' Neighborhood*, is really their hard work questioning, figuring out life. Poets and scientists are known for their childlike curiosity, their ability to keep open minds. "The key to continuing to make discoveries is the ability to keep the 'why' alive," said one scientist. The truth of things is so elusive, so mysterious and thick, even weird that it keeps beckoning us, seducing us, alluring us.

The late Scott Peck said it's not just cynicism or busyness that gets us stuck in life but laziness. When confronted with life's predictable crises we dig in, or keep to the routine, or burrow down. We avoid seeking new approaches, alternative routes and personal inquiry.

In their meeting Jesus said to Nicodemus, "For God so loved the world that he gave his only Son so that whoever believes in him will not perish but have eternal life." A resident in the world of the flesh would be baffled by that statement. But Nicodemus took a chance; he left the safety of his ivory tower. He asked, on the face of it, a silly question and that's the answer Jesus gave him.

I remember when I confessed confusion about my personal life and asked God, if there was a God, to help make sense of it. It was my first prayer as an adult. I was fifteen. Divorce and a death prompted me. The very question, 'Do you exist?' made me realize I was looking for a personal God, not an intellectual category or concept. I'd stepped into a new world. The old rules were too small. You could say I was 'born anew from above'. The same thing happened to Nicodemus. The next time he shows up is at the end of the Gospel with Joseph of Arimathea to take Jesus' body to be buried. The rigid old scholar was seeing this world as if for the first time. His willingness to look for Jesus one night, to risk looking foolish and ask some questions opened his eyes. My guess is some of us need to take the same chance. Amen.

The Importance of Trust: Dead or Alive
John 11:5-6

April 2, 2017

One of the great things about hard-to-understand poetry and abstract art is its inexplicability. Words and reason fall short of tagging, naming, and categorizing the subject matter such works deal with. So that we have to read the poem again and yet again; or step back from the painting or sculpture and let our minds go free of trying to answer the question what does it mean? As if in finding a quick and easy answer to that question we can then walk on to the next painting or sculpture to dissect and analyze it and in like manner "do" the gallery.

Yet, what the riddle of such art does is shake us loose from our neatly organized worlds and transport us to another space where our need to keep the anxiety caused by unanswered questions about life at bay is exposed and we find ourselves confronting a truth: the world is sometimes an enigma and defies our attempts to explain it. That we can be confused and forced to confront our limitations is not always a welcome experience. Today's story from John is like a confusing poem or painting.

The raising of Lazarus reveals that the world and human existence are more wondrous and surprising than we often see in our day-to-day lives, and perhaps even more wondrous and amazing than we are willing to accept. This is the Easter story and we will consider the bold challenge it makes to our linear, proof-based worldview in a few weeks.

But the portion of the story we heard this morning, that occurs before Lazarus is raised, offers another revelation: not only do we live in a world where raising people from the dead is unheard of, but our expectations of God as a loving deity and Jesus a compassionate Savior are challenged when Jesus strangely delays going to help Lazarus.

Jesus' choice to ignore the impending death of a cherished friend and grief of a family that have supported him from the beginning not only doesn't add up, it contradicts who we think Jesus is. I know the account goes on to tell us that Jesus says to his followers that Lazarus' illness is for the glory of God and that Lazarus hasn't really died because, though John hasn't yet informed us, Jesus will raise him, and therefore Jesus says Lazarus has only 'fallen asleep'; this statement amounts to either a cruel euphemism or the central and profound truth at the core of Christian faith.

Soren Kierkegaard was so fascinated by this story that he rewrote and retitled an earlier consideration of its theme in a work called *The Concept of Dread*, but after his conversion to Christianity prompted him to revisit the epic battle of death v. life in a work titled *Sickness unto Death*. Lazarus' sickness was *not* unto death because he was finally raised to life; but the real sickness unto death, says Kierkegaard, is human despair because it closes our hearts and minds to the Risen Christ.

The fact is Jesus knows that by the time they arrive at Bethany Lazarus will be physically dead, wrapped in grave cloths and sealed into a tomb for four days. When Jesus finally appears on the scene, Lazarus' grieving sisters are hosting a houseful of grieving friends, loved ones and synagogue members. Jesus' entrance to the house makes a 'scene' that from the larger strategy of the story is exactly what his late arrival is intended to do. Jesus consoles the sisters, is moved to tears himself, and which prompts others to say 'see how he loved him' as if to confirm that Jesus' delay wasn't because he didn't care about Lazarus. Jesus is then taken to the tomb and orders the stone to be rolled away and Lazarus to come out. At this point everyone shrieks because of the anticipated stench of a decomposed human body.

When Lazarus appears at the entrance to the cave, grave cloths dangling, everyone believes—Mary and Martha, who already knew that with Jesus anything was possible; but also friends and synagogue members—plus the disciples who weren't always ready to believe, nor sure what Jesus meant when he said Lazarus was only sleeping. A comment from Marilynne Robinson regarding how our secular, sound bite culture attempts to understand Jesus helps; Jesus, from her perspective, does not conform to the present impulse everywhere visible from the latest 'life for dummies book' to those who have turned organized religion into a self-help philosophy by shrinking and reducing what is complex to appease the multitudes and leverage profit.

The life of Jesus, Robinson writes, is very well attested by the standards of antiquity. *Yet, how he is to be understood is a question of another kind.* The essential point is that the demand for proof, as 'historians' of religion would have it, if it were made rigorously and consistently, would and has led to disappointing results. Yet, this by no means justifies the conclusion that whatever cannot be proved is, therefore, meaningless or false. Nor would it legitimize the burgeoning of fundamentalist truth claims that are themselves totally unprovable and that flourish in contempt of evidence. In fact, this kind of thinking is pandemic in contemporary society, and Robinson for one takes comfort, if a cold comfort, in the fact that many members of Congress participate in or defer to it (e.g., anti-science legislation); and so she feels free to use the traditional vocabulary of faith.[i]

Robinson writes that she is drawn to Calvin's description of the world as a theater, with the implication that a strong and particular intention is expressed in it, that its very limits and boundedness are meant to let meaning be isolated out of the indecipherable weather of the universe at large. She quotes John Locke to say that just because something is bounded, limited, or finite does not mean that human experience constrained by it is likewise limited, but rather can be empowered, expanded, extended.

Having proposed that all thought is based on four simple ideas, Locke warned his reader not to consider these simple ideas too narrow for the capacious mind of man...which takes its flight further than the stars. This from a British empiricist philosopher who, with a few others, gave birth to modern thought rooted in the human capacity for reason and logic, yet who did not discount or divorce himself from the mystery and wonder of the universe.

David Brooks wrote on Friday that we may be living in a world that has reached the twilight of its existence; a moral universe that has finally come unhinged from moral categories associated with traditional religious practice; and yet it is a world still fully possessed of what feels right and wrong although it does not possess the vocabulary rooted in religious practice to discern, debate and decide matters of moral and spiritual consequence.

Brooks is spot on. The spirit-clogging resistance to a transcendent God and faith in the western world may have entered the bloodstream in the Enlightenment but it congealed like a clot in the artery of faith in the nineteenth century and has caused a spiritual embolism in the late twentieth and twenty-first centuries. As Brooks writes in his article, our guilt has nowhere to go to be forgiven or atoned (vestigial religious concepts as outdated as the appendix) but lodges in what has become a widespread feeling or tumor of victimhood—because if I make myself a victim of the actions of some liberal or conservative ideology I no longer have to feel guilty; I can rant at political oppressors.

The Gospel of John comes to its great crescendo when Mary recognizes the man she thought to be the gardener as the Risen Christ on Easter morning. But we are not yet there. Which is why, here in late Lent, today's story is so compelling and relevant. If you have ever felt abandoned by God or let down by your faith, if you have ever been left with disappointment or betrayal in some circumstance where what you counted on or someone you counted on did not meet your reasonable hopes and expectations, then today's story is for you.

By any commonsense human accounting, Jesus' delay is incomprehensible, even inhumane. But perhaps this is just the point. Jesus does not act in accord with common sense or even by standards of what is generally regarded as humane. He and his revelation of God are unique, are once and for all, and are not subject to the standards of the science or the methodology of history.

When you stop and think about it there are other egregious delays in justice, in healing. From the time the Hebrews went into slavery in Egypt to the time they were delivered—400 hundred years, including forty years wandering in the wilderness; 400 years from God's last words in the Old Testament to the first words of the New—Stanley Hauerwas says Israel's faith was "a long training in being out of control" of their relationship with God, without despising God. Grace, which means gift, isn't grace if it is predictable, programmable, and on demand.

Maybe that's why God takes God's own good time to show up. One mother commented she was disappointed her son who'd attended church from early childhood was not a Christian yet. Her pastor responded, "God has God's ways of getting what God wants. Tell your son to keep looking over his shoulder as he moves into his 40's." Faith isn't just belief in something; it is belief coupled with the acknowledgment of our limits. It is coming face to face with our finitude that also recognizes that we are not in complete control of our circumstances; that what coming to faith may mean is that we just may choose to be 'out of control' and learn to depend upon God.

The philosopher Kierkegaard conducted his campaign against organized religion in a nineteenth century Denmark–not unlike our time–in which preachers attempted to make Christianity 'plausible', an effort that led to its 'domestication.' So that in Denmark where prostitution was legal, but practitioners had to be licensed, the state required those applying to show their baptismal certificates to be approved.

What the story today teaches us, if it teaches us anything, is that we can finally understand God at work in our lives only by letting go of our human resources and coming empty-handed to receive the gift of faith. There's no easy answer to the perplexing circumstances and riddle of today's story: Jesus strangely delays going to see his gravely ill friend Lazarus.

The people in the story don't have the benefit of seeing into the future to know how this will turn out. They are crushed by death. So are we. What the raising of Lazarus reminds us is that when that happens to us, even as it may be happening now in some of our lives, it's not the end of the story. Patience. Trust. God works in mysterious ways. Those are good words and practices to add to any spiritual vocabulary. Amen.

– Palm / Passion Sunday –

He Looked Around at Everything
Mark 11:1-11

April 1, 2012

We enter, today, the holiest season of the Christian year. Holy Week recounts a story that lives in the world not as history or myth but, said one writer, as "light, saturating light." The essence of the story is that God is of a kind to love the world extravagantly, wondrously, and the world is of a kind to be worth, which is not to say worthy of, this pained and rapturous commitment and sacrifice.

This is the Christian narrative, the story of Jesus the Christ. It begins with the scandalous birth and unfolds in the lives and hearts of the people as they are delivered from disease, listened to and cared for, and begin to comprehend the law and prophets not as tired accounts or rigid rules from long ago but as radical principles to guide their own living.

The story takes a turn when Jesus leaves the villages and hills of Galilee for the jaded and dangerous streets of Jerusalem. This light-infused epic culminates for Jesus in, of all things, an empty tomb after his execution by the state; but it starts for the disciples in a garden outside the tomb, in an upper room later that day and on the road to Emmaus as well; then at the lakeshore in Galilee where they had first met and decided to follow him.

That part of the story, after the empty tomb, is still being lived out and told in our own lives; and we come back like moths to the light, in disproportionate numbers, at Christmas and Easter—the two ironically most inexplicable moments of his life.

Why do we return? It is true that the story of Jesus of Nazareth can be "explained" in part from bibliographies and historical footnotes as well as research in the social sciences; but Jesus and his story are best grasped as light—enveloping, penetrating light that can be experienced but not defined. The essence of the story, the extravagant, wondrous God who utterly subjects himself to our dependably callous and violent behavior, this story and the players in it do not succumb to academic dissection and analysis. And because they do not, much of the story, indeed the most important parts of it remain shrouded in wonderment. The very thing we build our modern world upon—the continuities of history and calibrations of science—are for a moment fractured and the dismissive presumptions they support about religion and Jesus exposed. We return at Christmas and Easter because we are weary of the world's shrunken and predictable narrative of human life, and we hunger for a new, more expansive story and for light.

I want to explore with you today Part I, if you will, of this Holy Week saga: the entry to Jerusalem juxtaposed with the epistle reading from Philippians. The story begins with Jesus bouncing atop a borrowed donkey much like the picture on your bulletin cover or like a moped riding into the middle of a Harley-Davidson convention. It continues as he moves through the ecstatic, fickle crowd. But today's story ends as "Jesus entered into Jerusalem, and into the temple where he looked round about upon all things; but as eventide was come, he then went out unto Bethany with the twelve."

It is interesting that the epistle reading for the day begins with these words from St. Paul, "Let the same mind be in you that was in Christ Jesus." Could the lectionary committee have intended that we would associate the two—Jesus emptying himself, sitting atop a beast of burden, bouncing into the city, under the watchful eye of the occupation army and the religious authorities who had been in search of him and were plotting against him—is the committee suggesting that we too should empty ourselves of any claim to authority or power and place ourselves with Christ in the care and providence of God?

The circumstances in Philippi when Paul offers this guidance involved a dispute between competing factions in the church; Paul was urging the opposing parties to lay down their weapons and adopt the mind of Christ. But it was more than that too. For Jesus, and I suspect for those early Christians in Philippi, there were what could have been a host of issues and self-interests at stake. In the minds of nearly everyone—the disciples, the crowds, the religious authorities and the Roman governor—it was Caesar's power and control vs. the identity and sovereignty of the people. It was years of back-breaking labor and poverty vs. self-determination under the leadership of a charismatic rabbi.

You see, it wasn't just riding a donkey into town, it was aligning with the people along the lines of battle that had been drawn. That was the choice facing Jesus: to align himself with the timetable and interests of the people or to lay all that and the power that went with it aside and align himself with God.

The temptation in the wilderness comes to mind; the devil takes Jesus to a high place and says that he will give it all to Jesus if Jesus submits to his power and purpose. That temptation is a foretaste of this moment when he could have seized the power the crowds were willing to bestow if he served their ends.

It is worth noting that in his letter to the Philippians, Paul uses the word "epichoregas" in Chapter One to refer to the help to which he looks from the Spirit. "With the help of the Spirit of Jesus Christ, this will turn out for my deliverance." The deliverance he was referring to was an end to his imprisonment in Rome from which he was writing his letter urging the Philippians to lay aside their disputes. This word 'epichoregas' or help is used only one other time in the New Testament. It is the Greek word from which come the English words "chorus" and "chorale." Because the word implies "getting it all together," like a chorus singing in harmony; when the word is used in Ephesians, it is translated "being knit together." That's what a choral conductor does, he knits the singers all together.[1]

In Philippians Paul says, "I give thanks because I know that with the epichoregas of the Spirit of Jesus Christ, (with the choreography of the Spirit of Christ) this will all work out for my deliverance." Paul is in jail, yet even in chains he has faith in the choreography of the Holy Spirit. The Holy Spirit is the choreographer for our deliverance.

Some of us saw Neil Wechsler's brilliant adaptation for stage recently of an Ibsen play. It has ten acts, many sets, props and actors; the production had a choreographer who coordinated everything into a compelling drama.

The choreographer sees the big picture and all the moving parts; she understands the timing of the music and actors and dancers and plot of the story. That's what the Holy Spirit does—it coordinates the whole show. Paul could have said in his prayer, "God break these chains that bind me and make me free." But he didn't. Rather, he said, "with the epichoregas of the Spirit everything will work out." I'll bet that's similar to what Jesus prayed making his entrance to the city and later during the increasingly difficult days of Holy Week: "In your hands O God, with the epichoregas of the Spirit, I will get through this week."

So yes, that's my guess, the readings today are positioned not only to help us remember and celebrate Jesus' emptying himself; making himself obedient to the Holy Spirit; but they also come as an admonition for you and me to do as he did and trust in the choreography of the Spirit as we go about our lives. We are here today and through the days of this week not to observe Jesus but, as St. Paul said, to imitate him.

It's a tall order. Who among us does not pray to be delivered of something? We sit, like Paul, in our chains—of a health diagnosis or financial worry or concern for a loved one. Facing challenges, it is often tempting to see our lives in linear fashion as one move, then another and another. But, in fact, at any given time there are always lots of things going on. Indeed, there are an infinite number of possible factors that could affect a relationship or a diagnosis or a career. The little linear piece we are focused on that seems so important now may be a bridge or door or key to something more important later.

The past two Wednesdays we heard the stories of educator Keith Frome and Rabbi Gary Pokras; they told us how their lives unfolded in sometimes strange and unpredictable ways that led to their deliverance; to their decisions to work with children of poverty for Keith and for Gary to embrace his calling as a rabbi. The difference between letting the mind of Christ be in us or not is meeting life with caring detachment and acceptance; in being open to the choreography of our lives—even when things are bleak—and trusting that though we can't see where we are ultimately being led, God sees. When I am open and receptive like that to the events going on around me I feel lighter; more buoyant, more *radiant*—which is what the person meant who said that the story of Jesus lives not as history or myth, but as light, saturating light.

After we stop trying to control events swirling around us and trust God's choreography, as Annie Lamott says, "push up your sleeves and start helping. Every single spiritual tradition says we must take care of the poor, or we will be so doomed not even Jesus or Buddha can help us. We don't have to go overseas. There are people in this country who are poor in spirit, worried, depressed, dancing as fast as they can; their kids are sick, or their retirement savings are gone. There is great loneliness among us, life-threatening loneliness. We must do what we can, what good people have always done: bring thirsty people water, share our food, help the homeless, stand up for the underdog."[ii]

Martin Luther King, Jr. said, "Human progress never rolls in on the wheels of inevitability; it comes through the efforts of folks willing to be coworkers with God." Imitators of Christ.

When we feel imprisoned by fear or preoccupied by worry it helps to recall how Paul and Jesus trusted the choreography of God. We will probably never know what prompted Jesus on particular occasions to say or do particular things. But my hunch is when he reached Solomon's Temple after entering the city and went into the temple, as Mark says, and looked 'round about upon all things' I like to think that he was giving it all up one more time into the epichoregas of God. He was after all, as Paul says, a human being—which means, I trust, that he did not have any inside information as to how it would all turn out. All he had, all any of us have who long for some deliverance, is the ability to choose to empty ourselves yet again, put the problem in the hands of the master choreographer, then roll up our sleeves as Annie Lamott says.

No doubt more than a few of us could take a page from Paul's urging and Jesus' handling a tough situation; by letting go of the things we incessantly try to choreograph and control, focusing only on ourselves which in the end is all we ever can control, and instead by looking outward toward our neighbor and embodying the light. So as we enter our own Jerusalems this week, or sit like Paul in our own Roman prisons, let us have the mind in us that was in Christ Jesus. And offer radiance in a dark world. Amen.

[i] William Willimon, *Pulpit Resource*, April through June 2012, pg. 7.

[ii] Annie Lamott, *Plan* B.

– Maundy Thursday –

Calm Before the Chaos
1 Corinthians 11:23-26

April 13, 2017

When Paul wrote his first letter to the church in Corinth, from which tonight's lesson is taken, it was a church deep in conflict and dysfunction. Several groups within the congregation were in sharp disagreement over theological correctness and some were even divided along the lines of social class and status.

We're talking a mere generation and a half after Jesus walked the hills of Galilee. Of course, Moses had only been gone forty days on the mountain when he came back to find that the people had fashioned a golden calf and were engaged in an orgy of cultic worship and fertility rites. In utter frustration with their fickle faith and debauchery Moses smashed the tablets of the law, and who can blame him? But Paul, for his part, hearing of the discord in Corinth, channeled his frustration and concern into two epistles.

1 Corinthians is one of the great letters of the New Testament. Paul reminds these earlier Christians they are one community, not a collection of cliques; that diversity is a gift to be honored; that leaders need the contributions of followers; and he writes–in one of the most sublime passages of the bible– that the greatest gift to the church, what makes it work despite itself, is love. But before he enters into those topics, he does an inventory of the disconcerting reports about the congregation. He tells them again of the role of the church, and the rights of an apostle, then he turns to the Lord's Supper which in their practice has been an occasion for one-upmanship and drunken behavior.

One marvels that Paul had the patience; that he even believed they could be salvaged. Yet, this is where his letter segues into a timeless vision for the church. In three short verses he redefines for the Corinthians the sacrament of communion and the purpose of the church from a beer hall social club to an institution that aims for the transformation of the world. Paul takes them back to that night in the upper room when Jesus broke the bread and poured the wine. He gives them a firsthand report of that moment on the eve of the trial and execution when the world stopped, a calm descended, and they shared a simple meal together.

It reminds me of my first week at Yale Divinity School when the great Reformation historian Roland Bainton, then in his 80s, told us new students the story of the college and divinity school by recounting the contributions of the luminaries pictured in the portraits encircling the room. He started with Jonathan Edwards, America's greatest theologian, and ended with his own teacher and mentor Williston Walker pictured in a 1903 portrait of the faculty. When I walked into the room I was a nervous first year student— having left a small church-related Midwestern college for a major Ivy League institution. By the time Bainton finished speaking, I was part of a revered history, tradition and family of clergy, scholars and missionaries and the torch passed down from Edwards was now in our hands.

What Paul writes onto the hearts of the Christians in Corinth in these three short verses is that this supper Jesus gave us is both a memory and a proclamation. A memory because Jesus said when we eat the bread and drink the cup we are to remember him. The word 'remembrance' (anamnesis) appears in both the instruction for the bread and the wine; it says the Lord's Supper is part and parcel of and activated by the church's *memory of Jesus*. Jesus forged that link in the chain of memory in the upper room, when he said, 'when you do this remember me.'

We'd be lost without our memory; when a loved one dies, 'words of remembrance' in the service recall the particular details that made that person unique and special. We are admonished each year on Yom HaShoah to remember the Holocaust, lest history repeat itself. Memory is the life-line of civilization, as a guide for what we aspire to and as a warning for what we want to correct or avoid. When we eat the bread and drink the cup and remember the literal giving away of Jesus' life, we are fed by and become part of the same limitless love of God that was at work in his life. As the old saying goes, "we are what we eat."

But memory is not all, for the act of remembering is also a proclamation that in his sacrifice and death the power of life is unleashed. Paul writes: "as often as you eat this bread and drink this cup you proclaim the death of the Lord until he comes."

We are not just passive rememberers but partners, colleagues, and representatives of Christ. In the simple act of eating bread and drinking wine, we proclaim the same message Christ proclaimed that is the core of our faith. Which Peter said on Pentecost is this: "Jesus of Nazareth was handed over, crucified and killed. But God raised him up, having freed him from death because it was impossible to be held in its power." That was the first Christian sermon ever preached. Death is defeated. The good news we proclaim when

74

we eat the bread and drink the wine is because he died and was raised, those who give their lives away like him will be rescued from death like him; and if rescued then sent back into a death-dealing world to remember and proclaim Christ for the rescuing of others.

The sacrament of communion is not just an anniversary meal or excuse for a love feast turned blowout party as it was in Corinth. The sacrament of the Lord's Supper is the primary reminder and call to action that renews and refocuses the church for its work in a dangerous world. Petty divisions and social posturing are overshadowed by the cross; the business of the church requires a healthy, harmonious body of believers.

John Calvin said the celebration of the Lord's Supper is appropriate every time the community gathers for worship. It is the proclamation and pledge not just of the preacher but all who partake at the table to be as generous and extravagant with their lives as Jesus was with his. That we celebrate this supper tonight, on the eve of his death, realigns us with the cross and emboldens us with resurrection for the work of peace and justice in our time.

Not surprisingly the sacrament has been abused over the centuries. It has been regarded as a magical ritual that brings good luck and it has been made to seem so removed and holy that some churches observe it only once a year. You know the old story about the origin of the words "hocus pocus"–they refer to the Latin "Hoc est corpus meum," meaning, "This is my body"–the words of institution that the Roman church believed turned the bread and wine into the body and blood of Christ. Seventeenth century magicians bastardized the phrase into 'hocus pocus'–a sham invocation for their magic, mimicking the priests who turned the wine and bread into Christ's body and blood.

What we celebrate tonight is not magic or some removed and rare ritual or the occasion for social debauchery, but the galvanizing force for the people of God who live in the tension between Good Friday and the final day of history. There are varieties of theology for this sacrament–even within the Presbyterian Church, and I dare say among us tonight. I like Calvin's notion that the bread and wine somehow contain the real presence of Christ–a *mystical presence*–that wins the hearts of those who come to the table. There is a spirit of love and grace and healing here–especially on nights like tonight.

But whatever our theology, Paul was right; this meal is a memory and a proclamation–without which there would be no church. All hell did break loose when Judas got up and left the table. The temple police, the trial before Pilate and the chief priests, the crowd's demand for his death; his scourging

75

and carrying the cross, the nails driven into his hands and side and feet. Hell reared up when he seemed most vulnerable, like when he entered the wilderness and Satan appeared and the forces of darkness did their worst. But this supper in an upper room, in a quiet moment before the chaos, established their lifeline and our lifeline to the power of life in the days to come.

On the road to Emmaus, at the seaside, in countless gatherings large and small they remembered and proclaimed who he was, what he said and how he was raised from the tomb; and how it was now their turn to expose and defeat the same forces of darkness. From that table in an upper room so long ago to this table tonight, let us remember and proclaim who he is in these dangerous and challenging times. Amen.

– Good Friday –

When Violence Overtakes Itself
John 19:13-16

March 25, 2016

Video-artist Laura Poitras has an installation at the Whitney Museum of American Art. The first display is made of images filmed at Ground Zero in the days after the 9-11 attack. Little by little the viewer realizes the images are of people are looking at the remains of the World Trade Center in the first days after the attack. Poitras shows nothing but the faces which reveal the fathomless power and compulsion by which suffering and grief both isolates and unifies. There is a palpable sense of aloneness and loneliness as the images move in slow motion across the screen. We have seen the planes crashing and the buildings falling hundreds of times, but with what emotion? The look on their faces—overwhelmed, saddened, stricken—must be something like the look we had when we first saw the buildings burn and fall.

One man lifts a camera to take a picture of the rubble and finds he can hardly bear to do so. There is a turbaned Sikh, a young woman with an "I Love NY" button, a mother with her daughter. A slowed-down refrain from the national anthem, sung at Yankee Stadium before the fourth game of the October 2001 World Series adds to the film's white noise.

In the second video the sympathetic response is harder to find. A grainy, degraded black and white film shows, in the half-darkness, excerpts of an interrogation in Kandahar, Afghanistan after the retaliatory strikes by the US in October 2001. Two Arab prisoners are released from isolation into a room for questioning by American guards. The men kneel on the floor with bags placed over their heads that are repeatedly removed, then replaced by order of the guards.

You get the feeling the soldiers armed with rifles are killing time before the trained interrogators arrive. Overt brutality is visible in nothing they say or do. One of the remarkable features of the film is to witness the effects of violence close-up without the depiction of violence. Poitras wants to connect emotion with thinking and she seems to have concluded the spectacle of violence itself aborts thinking.

The third video projected onto the ceiling is more difficult to discern than the first two. It shows a night sky abundant with stars. These are the skies over the embattled tracks of Afghanistan. Eventually, military drones can be made out, then a subdued hum of voices is heard, the chatter of officers at the controls somewhere.

Finally, the order of the three installations makes sense: by terrible but predictable logic the pity shown by the people mourning at Ground Zero leads to the dank floor of the interrogation cell in Kandahar which leads to deployment of drones as the remedy from overwhelming emotion, loss, and grief.

Yet the eyes in the sky that look to save us and the war on terror present serious threats to our freedoms that include a technological trap from which escape is increasingly difficult and the mongering of fear by ambitious politicians. We are seeing the moral effects of organized cruelty.

If Maundy Thursday juxtaposes love and betrayal, Good Friday holds peace and violence side by side. What fascinates me after more than thirty years of preaching the Passion on Good Friday is its freshness and relevance. The story never gets old. In part, because humans—despite our remarkable gifts—are inherently flawed and broken; as Kant said, "Out of the crooked timber of humanity, no straight thing was ever made."

The story never gets old because while humans are fickle and broken, God is unendingly resolute and resourceful in pursuing us. Who would have thought just two generations after the end of WWII we would be witness in a presidential campaign to demagoguery reminiscent of fascist Italy and Nazi Germany?

The account of the Passion from the Gospel of John is a tightly scripted masterpiece of irony and reversal; the irony is that that those who presume to have power have no power at all, and those who pretend to be religious are spiritually bankrupt, while He who is weak controls the unfolding of events and the One scapegoated a criminal is the paragon of righteousness. The story takes us down and down into the depths of the human condition run amok. Those who orchestrate his death become victims themselves of the violence they perpetrate.

Two trials take place—one for Jesus with his appearances and questioning before the Sanhedrin, then Pilate, then Herod and then Pilate again—the other for Peter as he is given the opportunity to reveal his association with Jesus but denies his relationship three times. John's careful staging also indicts the ludicrous behavior of the religious people, preoccupied with eating the Passover lamb, but all the while preparing for the death of the Lamb of God.

Almost every scene exhibits some element of irony and incongruities that expose the true nature of Jesus and the feeble, pretentious schemes of the authorities and complicity of the people. The final irony occurs when Pilate brings Jesus outside the praetorium to face the crowd; he presents him to the people as "your King" to which the crowd responds they have no other king than the emperor, yet within hours, they will gather around their kosher tables and recite the liturgy that their only king is God, but here in order to reject Jesus they must reject God.

There is a scene from a Hemingway short story "The Snows of Kilimanjaro" in which the protagonist who has lived a life of lies despairs not because he has lied but because there is no truth left to believe in, which aptly describes the condition of the actors in this drama: so convinced that their power was the only truth and power worth believing in that, when at last it is exposed as fraudulent and vile, they have nowhere to turn no truth to hold on to. Judas' utter confusion and despair that causes him to take his own life no doubt represents the spiritual bankruptcy of more than just himself.

The conditions humans are wont to create when motivated by greed, prideful ambition, violence and fear ornament the histories of civilization. When a Holocaust survivor imprisoned at Auschwitz asked a guard, "Why all this? Why?" he was told, "There is no 'why' here." If you pressed them, if you pressed the crowds who stood beneath Pilate's balcony when he brought Jesus out to proclaim his innocence and asked them what crime he committed, if you asked the people who were there that day what reason Jesus was sent to the gallows and why they shouted over Pilate's appeal for justice and fair play, I suspect their answer would be similar to that of the Nazi prison guard.

Violence gives no real reason to exist—otherwise it would expose itself. All it requires is willing agents—those who will stomach the injustice and brutality levied against vulnerable and defenseless victims. One thinks of the scores of unarmed, innocent black men killed by police over the past several years; others come to mind—the Syrian refugees caught between the hell hole of civil war in the land they left and their mass herding in camps, now designated to Turkey, where food and shelter and health care are scant. And of course, there are the victims of terrorism in Brussels and Paris and Ankara just over these past few months.

Fred Rogers of Mr. Rogers' Neighborhood, commenting on child abuse, once said, 'Violence is a sign of impotence.' It indicates that the relationship, the dialogue, the mutual interest in one another has broken down and been abandoned. That analysis accurately describes the scene in the Holy City, this night 2,000 years ago, when Jesus was paraded before the people and condemned to die.

But, it was only one side that stopped the conversation and pulled back from the relationship—our side; as for Jesus he used up the last of his breath reaching out, saying, "forgive them for they know not what they do." The interval between creature and Creator is not diminished in this story, it is made absolute; and the unworthiness of the profane in contrast to Him is not extenuated but enhanced.

That God nonetheless admits access to Himself is not a mere matter of course—as we might presume it to be having heard this story so many times before—it is rather a grace beyond our power to comprehend. If the promise of God's final triumph reveals itself first and fully on Easter, it nevertheless presses to be seen even in the noon hour of Good Friday, for even here God does not abandon the people. Amen.

– Easter –

When Mystery Engulfs Reason
John 20:1-18

March 27, 2016

A few months ago, visiting Fort Bragg where our son is stationed, I made the mistake of taking pictures of the Joint Special Operations Command Headquarters–the nerve center for Navy Seals, Delta Force, the Green Berets and Army Rangers. My son quickly advised me to put the camera away–they don't like people taking pictures of that building he said, you could get us detained for questioning. You see, even though I was quite aware of being on Fort Bragg, I forgot for a moment–in a larger sense–where I was.

Understanding ourselves and the world makes all the difference in terms of how we go about achieving our personal goals and calling in life. And because we live in a technological age we defer to reason and quantifiable analysis to solve every problem. Our appetite for information is insatiable; research universities are the new cathedrals, we baptize graduates with advanced degrees for success in life–often defined as social status and material wealth. The myth of the apple in the Garden is that our hunger for knowledge disguises a deeper impulse–to be like God–which causes us to forget who we are, where we are, and why we are here.

The name for this is pride, intellectual pride–the greatest of the seven deadly sins. It has led, in our time, to misreading not just the purpose and depth of human experience but also the depth and nature of God. The imaginative story and myth of the bible, when dissected into its various sources, forms and cultic voices, results in the fundamental fact of religious experience about which those stories were told, then written, being, as it were, rolled out so thin and flat as to be finally eliminated altogether.

There is an old German saying, "Ein begriffener Gott ist kein Gott"–'A God comprehended is no God.' To affirm that the historical God is beyond the methods of science to explain and define is to wave a red flag in the face of the intellectual establishment of colleges and universities, and even some theological schools and churches. Small wonder then that there has been a rolling out and flattening of the human being–increasingly seen as but a series of incremental steps in the long march of evolution, our brains and appetites determined ages before when we were hunters and gatherers—our ethics and morality considered the product of our discovering the success of collaboration versus competition for preserving the species.

So writers and artists in Europe and America by the 1930s, Alfred Kazin says, started to despair. They stood face to face with the eclipse of the old sense of right and wrong that was founded on a belief in immortality (what today we call resurrection) and the final court of eternal justice. There was no longer a cosmic authority to keep the human heart from hopeless despair. Their stories had such titles as: The Trial, No Exit, The Plague, and The Man Who Disappeared.

Contributing to the malaise and despair, and to the epidemic use of pain killers and recreational drugs, are the treadmill of success and its accompanying mantra of consumerism, "I am what I own"; not to mention the wars we have sponsored—second to none in the history of civilization.

The 16th century philosopher Blaise Pascal describes the root of our fear and despair: "For it is clear beyond doubt that this life only lasts for a moment, that the state of death is eternal. "[i]

My purpose on this Easter morning is to probe the story of the empty tomb from the Gospel of John and consider what it tells us about the great orienting questions of life and how it answers Pascal's deepest questions about our purpose and destiny.

When Mary arrives at the tomb on Easter morning she is intent on one thing—going to the body of Jesus to conduct the ritual funereal preparation with herbs and spices. When she sees the stone rolled away she immediately, logically concludes the body has been stolen, for what else could she conclude? She runs to give this information to Peter and to the other disciple; when they hear her story they run to the tomb to see if Mary's information is correct; and they, too, see the stone is rolled away; Peter enters the tomb first, then the other disciple, and John says 'they believed', meaning they believed the veracity of Mary's story. The body had been removed, most likely stolen.

But Mary remained after the two left; for, as John says, they did not as yet understand the scripture that he must rise from the dead; indeed how would they understand such a prediction or conclude that that is what they were witnessing, so they go back to their old world. When Mary ventures into the tomb she sees two angels who seek to console her—for she is clearly distressed; then, when she turns around, she sees a man she assumes to be the gardener but who John tells us is Jesus; and in what would be a touch of humor were it not so tender Mary asks the man if he is the one who has removed the body and where she might go to find it.

At which point Jesus calls Mary by name and she recognizes him instantly because of the physical sound of *his voice* pronouncing her name; and we witness what is surely one of the Bible's most remarkable moments: like the legendary continent of Atlantis rising from the sea; or the moment Lucy leads her sister Susan and brothers Peter and Edmund through the wardrobe into the land of Narnia–it is the collapse of the old structures of plausibility as happened when Newtonian physics gave way to Einstein's reality that allows for the bending of time and space. It is a new world.

Jesus instructs Mary to go and tell the disciples that he is ascending to his Father and their Father, to his God and their God. And she goes, with haste, and announces these things to the disciples. Neither miracle, nor metaphor, nor magic, Mary's encounter with Jesus at the empty tomb can only be described as belonging to the realm of mystery. As such neither theologians nor scientists can explain what took place that morning for it is an event that can only be proclaimed. It is no surprise that the season of Easter continues for fifty days during which Jesus continues to appear to his friends–it takes that long for the news to sink in; for the disciples to get their bearings in the new land of Resurrection. Nor is it surprising that the first thing they do after that new awareness has settled into their hearts or rather their hearts have settled into it is to start the church on Pentecost.

The direct result of the Risen Christ, loose in the world, is the coming together of this new community whose sole purpose is the telling of this remarkable story and the proclaiming of this stunningly good news–the realm and power of death has been defeated.

If that is your calling and mission then you will tell that story in all the places where it needs to be told, where people are desperate for healing and hope; you will go to all the places where death keeps men, women and children in its icy grip: in prisons and hospitals and back alleys of cities; you will tell the story where poverty crushes children and the pursuit of material wealth destroys marriages and families; you will go to places like Flint, Michigan, and Ferguson, Missouri; and the city of Goma, Congo, where Jericho Road Ministries has asked us to join them in a medical mission for children who have lost their families in the Congo's ethnic cleansing.

And you would tell the story, as we at Westminster have told the story and proclaimed resurrection, on the West Side of Buffalo where new immigrants, whose children still remember living in UN camps, make new homes.

Proclaiming the story of resurrection is to proclaim and build the movement called the Kingdom of God; it is to celebrate the wonder and gift of human life, it is to do the brave work of justice and to witness the joyful healing of broken relationships; to proclaim resurrection is to answer the question of who we are and why we are here.

Marylinne Robinson says something like this: If His presence in the Creation asserts the human as a uniquely sacred and intrinsic aspect of Being, and his presence on earth surely does, then how are we to believe that he, call him Christ, call him God, would sweep the whole of our species, whom he has relentlessly sought to restore, out of existence, or into some sort of abyss? Rather glad reunion, to receive unto himself, beyond our capacity to fathom how, each of us unique, beloved, if flawed. [ii]

Or, Robinson continues, it is inconceivable that the God of the Bible would shackle himself to the worst consequences of our worst behavior. Rather the reach of Christ's mercy would honor the long road of human struggle and the full palate of human diversity. Maybe his constant blessing falls on those great multitudes who lived and died without any name for him, or for those multitudes who know his name and believe they have only contempt for him. C.S. Pierce said it would be most Godlike of God to love those least like himself.

Others have attempted to find the right words, to convey what this day must have been for Mary and what this day is, I daresay, for many of us here this morning. William James in his *Varieties of Religious Experience* comes as close perhaps as anyone recording from others' religious experiences what Mary must have felt in the garden when Jesus called her name: "The perfect stillness of the night," one believer told James, "was thrilled by a more solemn silence. The darkness held a presence that was all the more felt because it was not seen. I could not any more have doubted that He was there than that I was. Indeed, I felt myself to be, if possible, the less real of the two."

Or Alfred North Whitehead, one of the greatest mathematicians of his time, who writes, "Religion is the vision of something which stands beyond, behind, and within the passing flux of immediate things; something which is real, and yet waiting to be realized; something which is a remote possibility, and yet the greatest of present facts; something which gives meaning to all that passes, and yet eludes our apprehension." [iii]

Proclamation. Good news. Not formula or analysis or provable propositions. The crux of the matter of Resurrection is where we place our trust: in the verifiable conclusions of linear logic or in the Risen Christ? If you haven't seen him or felt his presence at the break of day or in the middle of the night, there are the fifty days of Easter that follow this glorious morning; when he appeared on a lonely road to two of his followers lost in their disappointment and grief; or on a deserted beach when the fishermen were returning one morning with their catch; and as one, late to the party, the great Apostle who never saw or knew him in the flesh but encountered the Risen Christ on the hard road of his professional obsession fueled by avarice and cruelty, veiled as righteousness and virtue.

The common thread to each and all of these is that they had no idea or expectation that he would walk into their midst to awaken the life within them; to give them a keen and often times burning sense of why and where they are in the world.

For those who encounter him, who hear him call their name, there is the response of Mary, "Rabbouni", meaning Teacher. And then the sound of footsteps running back to the others to proclaim, "I have seen the Lord!" Amen.

i Blaise Pascal, *Pascal's Pensees* (London: Harvel Press, 1962) 109.
ii Marilynne Robinson, *The Givenness of Things*, (Farrar, Straus, Giroux, New York: 2015).
iii. Alfred North Whitehead, *Science and the Modern World*, (New York: The Macmillan Company, 1925).

– Eastertide –

Love Bade Me Welcome
John 20:19-31

April 23, 2017

The men's book group to which I belong reconvened the other night after a five-year hiatus. We are a religiously diverse group: two Presbyterians, an Eastern Orthodox Christian, a Reform Jew, an Episcopalian and two Roman Catholics. The book that brought us together was George Orwell's *1984*. Someone said, and I would agree: 'the book is not a great read but a scary experience to read.' We spent more time talking about the current environment of national and world politics than the book itself, which was, we thought, a sign of Orwell's relevance for today. *1984*, as you may recall, is about altering the values, beliefs and actions of people. So the conversation veered from politics into religion; at one point the Orthodox Christian among us raised his hand and asked the question, "Does a person *have to* believe in redemption and resurrection to be a Christian?"

Today's Scripture lesson is an answer to that question. All of us around the table agreed, for the most part, if we are told, per a totalitarian state or dictator, that we *have to* think or say or do something, we are likely to think, say or do the opposite. What is distinctive about the Christian gospel is that it is designed to spread the faith by persuasion, not fiat or dictate. Of course, there are some religious communities that assume complete authority and dictatorial power over people's lives—fundamentalist churches typically depend upon and enforce everyone's believing the same blueprint theology.

Presbyterians, however, have long protected the right of clergy and members to hold "scruples" to the essential tenets of faith. When the conservative wing of the church in the 18th and 20th centuries sought to require clergy to sign a document that pledged adherence to the essential tenets of faith, the legislative body could not even agree what the essential tenets of faith were.

Roman Catholics have more freedom than is typically perceived. One of the Roman Catholics in our group gave us some insight as to how this works for him on the issue of abortion/freedom of choice. He uses a Jesuit lens to ask himself questions that move from the theoretical realm, where he comes up with one answer, to the practical realm of applying his answer, and finds himself contemplating a different and opposed answer. This person works for a prominent Catholic institution and has frequent interaction with the bishop yet holds no lock-step position on tough issues.

When John sits down to record his account of Jesus' life he is not a dictator. His gospel is a series of increasingly remarkable signs that reveal Jesus is who he says he is—from turning water to wine, to healing a lame man, to giving sight to a blind man, to raising Lazarus and finally being raised from death himself. John seeks to convince the reader through a series of revelations that inspire deeper trust.

But let's come back to Orwell for a moment. The specter of *1984* hangs over today's world. Last week I stumbled onto live streaming of North Korea's three-day celebration of the founding dictator's birthday. The assembly of troops and armaments was designed to convey the monolithic power of the state. The messaging from the speakers, including the dictator, was eerily close to that of Big Brother in Orwell's dystopian novel. I got the sense there is zero tolerance for anything but the party line. Though, admittedly, like *1984*, since the state controls the press and media, it is unlikely that any narrative, message or account other than official party line ever reaches the people.

This hardline control does seem to be a global trend. Perhaps you saw David Brooks' article last week. He writes about the crisis of what the last generation called "Western civ". This was a narrative about the development of civilization as an accumulation of great ideas and innovations from the Egyptians, through Athens, the Magna Carta, the Age of Faith and the Renaissance and the Declaration of the Rights of Man.

The Western civ narrative came with certain values about the importance of reasoned discourse, the importance of property rights, the need for a public square that was religiously informed but not ecclesiastically dominated. It set a standard for what great statesmanship looked like and gave diverse people a sense of shared mission, a common vocabulary and a framework within which political debate and argument could help identify common goals. But a few decades ago many in the academic community lost faith in the narrative of Western civilization. Now if it is encountered at all it is presented as a history of oppression. The consequence of this erosion and rejection, Brooks writes, is the rise of illiberals and authoritarians who not only don't believe in democratic values but don't even *pretend* to believe in them as former dictators did.

We are leaving the age of reasoned, consensus-building leaders and entering the age of the strongman—witness the shift in Russia, Turkey, Egypt, and the doubling down of China and North Korea; plus the wave of nationalist parties and leaders in France and Germany; not to mention the United States. Last week was the debut of John Kelly, Secretary of Homeland Security, who positioned his department, in his first public speech, for the swift and un-relenting crack down of immigrants and Muslims justifying across the board guilty-until-proven-innocent vetting and restrictions—including the separation of mothers and children entering the country, which Secretary Kelly proclaimed was already proving effective in deterring would-be migrants.

Maybe things are closer to the first century than we realize when people like Caesar Augustus and Nero or Herod and his sons ruled with unlimited, unilateral power; and religious authorities required strict adherence to rules and observances that negated allowing the spirit of the law to take precedence over the letter of the law should a human life or some matter of justice hang in the balance. Unbridled power corrupts whether in the first or twenty-first century.

Enter today's lesson from the Gospel of John. It's worth noting that John's chronology of resurrection, ascension, and Pentecost is different from the Luke/Acts chronology of those events and is the commonly observed sequence in the church.

In John's account, Jesus is raised on Easter, when he appears to Mary in the garden, and he tells her he is *ascending* to his father and her father; then he appears to the disciples and tells them he is *giving them* the Holy Spirit (the moment of Pentecost in Acts); then he commissions them with the authority to forgive—or not to forgive—the sins of any they encounter.

Luke/Acts tells us that Jesus was raised on Easter, ascended to the right hand of God in heaven forty days later and ten days after that the Holy Spirit descended on the disciples at Pentecost; which we refer to as the birthday of the church, when the community of faith was empowered by the Holy Spirit to carry out the mission of Jesus with his authority to teach, heal and administer the forgiveness of sins.

What John is accomplishing with his condensed chronology is the coalescing and commissioning of the church on the day of resurrection. Though the word *ekklesia* or "church" does not appear in the Fourth Gospel, from beginning to end the narrative makes clear that the Christian community finds its model and mandate in Jesus himself. Despite the challenges of keeping old members, attracting new ones and motivating people to participate, the church is different from other social groups. Its reason for being is not in its apparent successes or failures, in its growth or influence, but in the call and commission of Jesus.

I mention this because it expands what John tells us happened in the upper room on the first Easter and then again a week later when Thomas was present. Jesus is appearing to and commissioning his church. This is important lest we think faith is a privatized experience that matters only to me. Rather it is a communal enterprise in which the community is charged to carry the message to the world and to take a stand for justice wherever there is injustice—just as Jesus did.

What would it take to convince those disciples, to convince Thomas, to enlist in this movement that became the church of Jesus Christ? They lived in a day and age of dictators, rulers and religious authorities with unlimited power. They were used to the leader of the occupation government dictating what they were and weren't allowed to do, from paying taxes to the right of assembly to their professed belief in a deity. Could they comprehend any other system of governance, of leadership; could they even conceive that *they had a place* in the decision-making process?

Jesus understands this. His ministry is gentle; he invites people to come as they are, to listen, to take what they want and leave the rest. To the rich young man searching for eternal life, when pressed, Jesus offers a remedy—sell what you own, give the proceeds to the poor, and then follow me; the man chooses to decline. Jesus heals people who ask to be healed and tells them it is *their* faith, *their* willingness that makes healing possible. It is not so surprising that the early church developed a communal, shared form of power and decision-making.

What is so radical about the emergence of Christianity in the first century is that Jesus bases his kingdom and rule upon "agape" love; that is love directed outward to the other. By its very nature such love can only be shared and accepted by invitation and persuasion, not decree and mandate. Jesus tells the disciples as much in the upper room when he washes their feet—he shows them disciples m this love in action, how it humbles and lowers itself; how the one who is master becomes servant.

The choir will sing today Ralph Vaughn Williams' setting for the poetry of George Herbert—a seventeenth century Anglican priest—who wrote religious verse; Herbert's perspective is what used to be called 'the man in the street.' What motivated Herbert to write poetry was his own falling short of a Christ-like life; he knew he was not alone; and he believed that a robust faith was grounded in a personal relationship with God, yet expressed in active service to others. Herbert's model for his love poems is a friend talking with a friend– the religious version of the Socratic method of question and answer to arrive at the truth. Yet, the voice in Herbert's poetry is no abstract, theoretical Lone Ranger but a full-fledged, card-carrying member of the church. You could say Herbert's poetry is theological inquiry for the application and benefit of the people of God.

What is striking about Mystical Song III — "Love Bade Me Welcome"— is the unrelenting pursuit of love to win the one guilty of dust and sin. Love meets us, Christ meets us, as he meets Thomas today in the upper room, at every turn with humility and generosity, giving us the benefit of the doubt; ready to sacrifice anything until we accept and experience the whole and abundant life he offers. What finally happens is that love conquers the fortress of the human heart–not by force, like a dictator, but by relentless, honest invitation to those who live in darkness to 'taste and see.'

Do we have to believe in redemption and resurrection to be a Christian? The question is not so much 'do we have to' as 'do we want to'; love gives us reason, over and over, to trust that we are indeed unconditionally accepted by a great and gracious God regardless of our past; and therefore redeemed, liberated from the mistakes and shame that still hold power over us, yet suddenly lose their grip and fall away.

The burden of guilt lifted, *we are raised* from the tombs of despair and regret and resentment that bound us. No dictator, no power of state, or force of arms can accomplish that. Amen.

More New Life
Acts 9:36-43; Revelation 7:9-17

April 17, 2016

Today's lesson from Acts depicts Easter, like June, busting out all over. That's the way it is with Easter and the fifty days following—new life everywhere; new life where you least expect it; like the greening of Buffalo's streets and yards this April. The reading from Revelation—also an Easter text—is an answer to the question asked earlier in chapter six, "For the great day of wrath has come and who is able to stand?" To which today's reading in chapter seven replies, "The great multitude who have come through the ordeal, robed in white, washed clean by the blood of the Lamb, who fall upon their faces at the throne and worship God singing praise and blessing." Both readings proclaim the victory of life over the realm of death. These were then, and are now, proclamations that bring hope and strength to the marginalized and oppressed.

Here it is week four after Easter; part of me wonders if we can stand that much good news, that much new life. We live in a world accustomed to daily doses of bad news. Witness the presidential campaign—a circus of audacious, offensive pronouncements by those vying for the highest office in the land. Or news from the international front—we see the headlines; we hear the drum beat of terrorism and violence, corruption and fraud. So here we are for the fourth Sunday in a row hearing how all those forces of darkness get defeated, one after the other; tamed, put in their place; defanged; negated; silenced.

This is news either too good to be true or so good it has to be true. The arch over this chancel depicts the implements of death used to kill the first Christian martyrs. Consider, for just a moment, what they were thinking when Dr. Holmes proposed that those symbols hover over the chancel and communion table. The audacity, the confidence to post the worst of the evildoers; as if to say, "is that all you have?" Reigning over the communion table in a Roman arch joined at the peak by a cross where the sign of Caesar would appear. A cross, used to execute the pioneer and perfecter of our faith, the risen Christ. The cross, transformed into a symbol of life—his body and blood freely given; as if to say, 'there are no limits, qualifications or conditions on God's love; not even death can thwart, stop, or turn it back.'

91

Tabitha is the only female in the New Testament referred to as a disciple; her resurrection announces that the risen Christ is alive and at work in the ministry of the apostles.

Tabitha was a Dorothy Day of the Catholic Workers movement; or Mother Theresa, or Rosa Parks; poor herself, standing up for the poor and oppressed. Her loss was the loss of a folk hero; a Roberto Clemente killed in a plane crash taking medical supplies to Nicaragua suffering from the devastation of a hurricane.

The raising of Tabitha is amazing in a patriarchal world; this story of a woman who is honored and remembered for her leadership and activism on behalf of others in need is a dramatic exception to all other historical records. What sort of community is this that breaks barriers, where women lead, and where people are cared for who are not members of one's biological family? Something strange and out of the ordinary must account for such a countercultural community. We know by now, in Eastertide, this strange, out of the ordinary something must be named "resurrection."

Tabitha's ministry? She makes clothes for the poorest of the poor; caring for those whom no one else cares for—those who are invisible to the rest of society but who, to her, were God's suffering, precious children. Imagine if you were one of those poor ones; you could not afford clothes or did not have adequate clothing. Reed Taylor's aunt Dorthea Lange, one of America's great photographers of the early 20th Century, chronicled them—the rural poor during the Great Depression. Or James Agee and Walker Evans' Depression era book, *Let Us Now Praise Famous Men*, that depicts in words and pictures poor white southern share croppers, families with small children, all of them—adults and children—dressed in tattered dirty rags.

Agee describes in his searing prose a typical 'family' as he came across them in his Alabama travels; "This family must take care of itself; it has no mother or father; there is no other shelter, nor resource, nor any love, interest, sustaining strength or comfort, so near, nor can anything happy or sorrowful that comes to anyone in this family possibly mean to those outside it what it means to those within it. It is, as I have been told, inconceivably lonely, drawn upon itself as tramps are drawn round a fire in the cruelest weather; and thus and in such loneliness it exists among other families, each of which is no less lonely, nor any less without help or comfort, and is likewise drawn in upon itself. Such a family lasts, for a while: the children are held to a magnetic center: then in time the magnetism weakens, both of itself in its tiredness of aging and sorrow, and against the strength of the growth of each child and against the strength of pulls from outside and one by one the children are drawn away."[ii]

Imagine what a Tabitha would mean to someone in that family, someone who provided you with new, fit, clean clothes and who understood your struggle and plight and took pains to reach out to and welcome and comfort you and members of your family; and imagine the impact of Tabitha's community of likeminded folk, caring for one another like family, sharing all they had, yet but not being blood relations. It would mean life where death was making its slow and inexorable claim. It would mean waking up into a new day of less loneliness, less hunger, less fear. Death is physical, but it is spiritual too–the loss of hope and energy and resolve; the end of vision, dreams and laughter.

Tabitha and her community were vigilantes against the darkness or the loss of trust and faith in the system; whether the health care system or educational system or economic system. We saw *The Big Short* a few nights ago–based on the true story of the 2007 fiscal crisis. That's a loss of life and hope that we can relate directly to; 40% of this church's invested funds gone; a budget cutting process in the years following that mirrored the ones going on in many households in this community and across the nation. Lost jobs, lost retirement, lost dreams.

Yet the message today is that death does not have the final word. Peter's "Tabitha get up!" reminds us of the way Jesus evoked the dead Lazarus from his tomb. Surprise! Jesus' disciples have the same power over death Jesus has. If you thought Easter happened once back in April, think again.

The Easter commotion continues. A woman in a small-town church hears a local politician rant about American Muslims and invoke his Christian faith to condemn them. She writes a letter to two Muslims in the company where she works. She expresses repulsion at the words of the politician and says she knows how they must feel when they see hateful jihadists on television using her beloved religion to justify terror and death. Or perhaps you remember hearing about the group of church women in North Carolina–a state maligned in recent days for the politics of its governor–these women wrote letters to mothers in Iraq, expressing their sorrow at our country's actions, showing concern for the suffering that Iraqi mothers and their children were going through. "We have no idea what difference our letters will make," said one, "but we are convinced it's what Christ expects and if we do what we can do, he'll take our offering and do the rest." Another group of women in an upstate county regularly take freshly baked chocolate chip cookies to the county jail, hand them to people incarcerated there and watch as those cookies are miraculously transformed into an overflowing of God's love and life even in that house of hate and death. Easter commotion: Tabitha is alive and well.

We'll talk this afternoon about the text from Revelation. Yet another biblical account of new life; the heavenly choir referred to in the reading we heard this morning; they sing God's praise and glory, for these were the ones who were persecuted and martyred under the reign of terror presided over by the Roman emperor Nero. Talk about losing faith in the system; talk about the forces of darkness having full sway over the circumstances of life. These Christians were driven underground into the Roman catacombs. Yet, they surfaced to serve and care for the sick, the poor and the hopeless. To be Christian then was to be a martyr; that was the definition of faith.

The opening of the seven seals in the book of Revelation is nothing short of a final victorious shout of Alleluia in the closing pages of the bible's sixty-six books and six-thousand-year history from the call of Abraham to the ascension of Jesus. I hope you can join us this afternoon as we hear a nearly 100 voice choir sing the Easter claim to resurrected life.

In the meantime, here's the message this morning: the test of the faith of our congregation is not how glorious and impressive a service we had on Easter; the test is what happens here in our church and here in our community for the poor and outcast because of our church, just four Sundays later. Amen.

[i] James Agee, *Let Us Now Praise Famous Men* (Houghton Mifflin: Boston: 1939) 50.

– Pentecost –

Imbibe
Acts 2:1-20

June 8, 2014

My wife has a way of getting my attention. If I am into some zone of moodiness or poor-me thinking she comes from behind me puts her hands on either side of my head, above my ears, and starts messing up my hair. Invariably this works. It provides enough distraction that I am knocked out of the rut I am in and start laughing as she is laughing and the fixation of 'leave me alone' or 'the world is out to get me melts away and I start speaking a whole new language of cooperation and affection.

That's what happened on Pentecost; just as I get loosened up and launched in a new direction with a change of heart, so when the Holy Spirit descended upon the disciples they too got stirred up, spun around and when they were set down again their old attitudes and fears like weights had fallen away; they started talking enthusiastically with a new vocabulary of vision and purpose.

Here's another way to see it. Pentecost Sunday is commonly referred to as the birthday of the church. It marks the end of the season of Holy Week and Eastertide and the beginning of something the world had never seen before. If Eastertide and the resurrection appearances are the formation of the spiritual embryo that is birthed on Pentecost, then we find ourselves in the birthing suite today. The time of gestation is over. We have this new arrival, the infant church. The Book of Acts is the diary of the infant church: "took first step", "said Mommy", "waved to Daddy." The disciples are aware of a new collective identity; they are the body of Christ, the hands and feet, the arms and legs of Jesus. Like an infant discovering its appendages they discover the animating power of the Holy Spirit; they start flexing their muscles preaching, teaching and performing miraculous acts of healing.

Or finally you could see Pentecost as the founding of a new republic: there are a lot of speeches in the Book of Acts. Like the new republic of the United States of America, telling the world through its Declaration of Independence, Constitution, and Bill of Rights about a new world view; a new way of seeing common citizens and exercising political power, the disciples start telling the world a new way of seeing God and understanding our relationship with God and one another. No entity with such a vision or purpose had ever existed.

95

They were disparate, fragmented and weak like the American colonies. But this burst of Holy Spirit galvanized the disciples and propelled them to the ends of the earth with their new worldview. It is unthinkable that they would have even thought of leaving Palestine without the Spirit pushing and leading them. Like the birth of democracy, there was the sense in the early church that they were part of something bigger that would change the world.

It's interesting that those who witnessed this event thought that the disciples were drunk. But Peter reminds the crowd that it was only nine in the morning. Yet, something about their behavior made some observers think intoxication. *They were drunk* but they were drunk on the Spirit of God. A Korean War veteran tells how he learned to drink as a soldier in that war. "Who can go into battle, face the enemy and risk being killed without a couple of stiff drinks?" he asked. You could say the same thing about the battle we are engaged in: the showdown against the forces of darkness wherever it rears its head. That's what Jesus calls us to do; to take on the demons that cause injustice, oppression, despair, hunger, and violence; and to care for those still living in the grip of fear. Tough assignment! If you and I don't need some outside spiritual bolstering, like that Korean War veteran when he went into battle, then I wonder if we are really responding to the tough demands Jesus places upon us.

In fact, you can see the bolstering power of the Spirit at work in the mission of this congregation. Serving on the board of the Westminster Economic Development Initiative I have seen that board and those leaders take huge risks. We'd pray at every meeting and we weren't just going through the motions; we were asking God for a good stiff belt of Holy Spirit to see us through, to help us make this thing work against all odds. The failure rate of new businesses is staggering! The leap from being church-supported to self-sustaining was like being on the motorcycle at the circus that zooms off a ramp and flies over a fire pit below to a ramp on the other side and a safe landing. I recall more than one meeting feeling like we were in mid-air and it was a long way down, praying that we had enough momentum to reach the other side. "Give me another shot of Holy Spirit," I'd pray, "to steady my nerves."

Or our Re-entry Friends. These folks are learning how to offer the right kind of help to men who have been incarcerated in some cases for years and who want to take the first baby steps to a new life. You can't do it with just good intentions. Sometimes you say the right thing, sometimes the wrong thing; sometimes your ex-offender asks for more than you can give or sometimes they just go off the grid and don't return calls. It takes courage to enter into a relationship like that—and a few good belts of Holy Spirit.

I am not lobbying for us to become alcohol dependent people; alcohol has wreaked enough havoc. What I'm talking about is becoming a Holy Spirit dependent church. Pentecostals get this better than Presbyterians. Jesus is always present, but no one should expect the Holy Spirit to help them walk on water if they refuse to step out of the boat. So, if you're sitting, you need to stand; if you're standing, you need to clap; it you're clapping, you need to dance; if you're dancing, you need to shout. Take the first step, let the Spirit take over!

One way of doing that today is to fill out that Pentecost card in your bulletin. Put some tangible action or goal down. Get out of the boat! A clergy friend shared an experience he had visiting what he called an aggressively buttoned-down, staid church. The congregation was in decline, the pastor was depressed and asked my friend, "What am I going to do?" And my friend had this thought: "Here's what you should do. Go out and buy 180 gallons of wine–it happened before at the wedding in Cana when Jesus provided the refreshments for a sagging wedding bash–though straight grain alcohol might be better–and pour it down the throats of this stiff and staid congregation. Maybe that will help." A good jolt, bolt, belt of the Spirit is sometimes what it takes. Fighting the forces of darkness that are often embodied in institutional attitudes and habits of thinking small and avoiding risk can get you branded a trouble maker or dreamer.

We're attempting something very big here at Westminster, we are attempting to change the culture of this community. We're attempting to make a paradigm shift from practicing our faith out of duty and obligation to practicing our faith out of gratitude and generosity. One of the saints of this congregation, Mary Kent Prentice, joined the company of heaven last week. Maybe you were here Thursday for her memorial service; the place was packed. She was 90 years old. She lived her life with gratitude and generosity. She served the church in countless ways; she involved herself as a volunteer and leader in more organizations than I have time to name; and she did little things like taking a plate of cookies or a poem with her husband Pren to someone who had lost a loved one or just got back from the hospital or was merely feeling low.

You don't operate that way if duty is all that motivates you. It takes more than obligation to animate a life. It takes the presence of God's Spirit. And it's contagious, like fire. Delivering a plate of cookies to someone out of obligation or out of joy and gratitude *look the same* but they *feel much different* to the recipient. That's the shift our Ministry of Generosity Committee and our elders are asking us to consider. But we have to get out of the boat first. *The Spirit will come*; the bible makes that very clear. Jesus said, "I will send you the

Holy Spirit who will teach you everything and remind you of all that I have said. Do not be afraid."

Pentecost. Here's one more way to see it: they were having a nice church meeting with a good multi-cultural turnout, discussing by-laws. Then someone said, "I want to make an amendment to amend the motion." Just going through the motions, all so orderly and decent and dull. Then suddenly the place was on fire! The Spirit was cascading down. People were filled with 200 proof Holy Spirit of God. They started babbling, talking, hearing. A crowd gathered outside the meeting room. "Look! They're doing what Jesus was doing when he was with them. They must be drunk." "Not at all," Peter said, "it's nine in the morning!" But let's be honest, they were drunk: drunk on the possibilities of a new world; drunk on the possibilities for life. Amen.

-Trinity Sunday –

Create
Genesis 1:1 - 2:4a
June 15, 2014

Last Monday I had the unusual opportunity of boarding America's oldest active fireboat–the Edward M. Cotter–docked across the street from Swannie House–Buffalo's second oldest, on-going tavern. The façade of Swannie's has been beautifully restored, although I understand the sawdust on the floor inside may still be from the Nineteenth Century.

The Cotter also doubles as an icebreaker; and is indeed a very serious vessel. Four twelve-cylinder diesel engines roar from the engine room two decks below. The heavy gauge of steel for the ship includes a "belt" of Swedish iron for icebreaking. The cleats to tie the Cotter at dock must weigh three hundred pounds each and were probably made right here at Bethlehem Steel or Buffalo Forge.

We were headed to Silo City, a mile upstream. To make our way, operators raised two bridges so we could pass underneath. The journey along the Buffalo River took us through a canyon of soaring twelve to fifteen story grain elevators on either side of the river, once served by rail lines. Our host calculated that just one section of elevators held enough Midwestern wheat to make 1.5 billion sandwiches in 1900.

Though I spend most of my days less than a few miles from this historic former center of Great Lake commerce and industry, I had only heard and read about it. To see the physical mass of those structures, sail the iron-clad Cotter and see its water cannons firing fore, aft and mid-section as we did that night takes your breath away.

One of the first things several of us commented on as we steamed up the Buffalo River on a balmy June evening was that the nation doesn't do that kind of heavy industry manufacturing anymore. We are masters of services and computing, systems and strategies. Careers and fortunes are made on derivatives, mergers, acquisitions, apps and intellectual property. We don't make "things." Much of what is made is made elsewhere. One wonders if we would remember how to manufacture anything out of steel, glass, wood or plaster.

Today is Trinity Sunday, the day on which we celebrate the three-part nature of God. The lesson today is the opening of the grand story of Scripture, "In the beginning when God created the heavens and the earth." Note that the story begins with God, not with us. God is Creator, we are creatures. We don't create our existence, the world, or ourselves, God does. Psalm 100 proclaims, "Know that the Lord is God. It is he that made us, and we are his; we are his people and the sheep of his pasture." This affirmation goes against most of what we have been taught about ourselves in the modern world. We are urged to be self-creators, fabricating our own lives through our choices and decisions. But Christians, Muslims and Jews regard humans as the result of not just our own acts of creation but of God's continuing creation with us.

It would be interesting to consider how the shift from heavy industry and manufacturing to a service economy and management of human and financial resources has changed our self-perception. My hunch is that when we were primarily a manufacturing economy we may have had a more intimate knowledge of the relationship between Creator and creature. Creating something is a combination of design and purpose. It requires vision and material. Manufacturing depends upon a system of interdependent participants who work together to make things.

When I was in college I worked in a steel mill in Pittsburgh. I had a minimal role—emptying the huge box into which scrap fell from red-hot ingots being "rolled" into thirty-foot bars. If the scrap box wasn't emptied the rolling couldn't continue, which meant the ingots couldn't be poured from the foundry furnaces that melted iron ore into steel. I wasn't an executive in the company or a foreman in the plant, but I had an important part to play in a vast system, a company that was part of a larger industry and nation comprised of management, unions, related industries—an eco-system of communities and organizations focused on making things.

Yet, much of the practice of contemporary religion focuses on us as consumers rather than participants with God in shaping the world God wants. In the consumer economy the focus shifts from a communal, production-oriented society to the lone individual inventing himself or herself by myriad choices from a plethora of options that seek to satisfy personal preference while defining one's public and private self through the products we select.

Polls say most Americans still believe in God as Creator; that the earth didn't just happen but is the result of some sort of external, divine involvement. But that's where many contemporary relationships with God end—in the mists of creation, in the primal past; rather than with God continuing to be present and at work with us shaping the world.

But here's a surprise: Genesis says that creation isn't finished. The Hebrew verb "God created..." is not only past tense but is also continuing. The reading Claude shared this morning tells us God is still creating. Creation–you and I, this church and community, the human family and world are still a work in progress. It is the on-going creating God is doing with you and me, his co-creator creatures, imprinted with his image on our hearts that finds traction in our present and offers hope for our future. This is a long way from the Eighteenth-Century Watchmaker God of Deism who got everything started, and then disappeared from the scene.

A better translation might be "In the beginning, as God began creating," rather than suggesting creation is done, fixed and finished. One writer uses the analogy of a musician creating a piece of music; if God ever stopped creating, creation would end. God is constantly creating as the musician is constantly playing to make music. You and I, God's people, might be the chorus or the rhythm section playing God's (not our) melody or, better, God's symphony of truth and justice.

So, the question on this New Member/Glynda S. Taylor Organ Scholar dedication Sunday is this: What is God creating here at Westminster with you and me? Another way to look at it might be that God equips us to do the work God calls us to do. How are we being equipped today? Toward what end and purpose? One answer might be we're being equipped to extend the reach of our music ministry to include the education of future church musicians. Another answer resides in the hearts of John Patrick, Candace and Anna whom we received into membership in this church family. Something we're doing here attracted them; what piece of that ministry or any of our ministries are they being called to embrace, to further shape and offer to this community? In fairness they may not yet have answers to that question, so don't recruit them for your committee today at the coffee hour, but I hope and trust they will soon be able to answer the question just as I hope and trust any of us could answer the question–"What is God calling me to do here?"

It's fine to hang your hat for a while if that's what you need; to recover, rest, and heal from life, that's what congregations are for as well. But at some point, we are co-creators with God and called to do more than hang our hat. We are called to make something of this church and community. It reminds me of the spinning instructor I encountered once in another city. Just before I entered the room someone warned me that this spinning instructor was hardcore, the real deal. Indeed, when he started—and by the way there was not one empty bike in the room—he said in a gravelly, drill sergeant voice, "This is called a 'workout' not a picnic, not playtime, not a stroll in the park. My job is to make you work, to make you sweat, to push you till it hurts, no pain, no gain!"

This entity Westminster, the church, is also called the 'body of Christ in the world.' We're not the memory of Christ or the idea of Christ. We are the body of Christ. God formed the church on Pentecost. We are the hands, feet, legs, and arms of Christ. Our purpose is to bring the kingdom of peace and justice into a warring, broken world. What that looks like in Buffalo, what that looks like in your life and my life is not just up to us; it is up to the Creator to whom we belong and who brought the world, the church and us into being.

John Montague, our renowned maritime scholar, painter and shipbuilder, was on the Cotter the other night. He told the story of a man in Rochester who bought his original painting of the Cotter and four prints for his four adult children. "The Cotter rescued my father," the man said, "from a burning vessel before I was born. I wouldn't be here were it not for the Cotter; that's why I want the painting and I want my children who also wouldn't be here were it not for the Cotter never to forget that either," he said. You and I wouldn't be here were it not for the Creator who brought creation into being long before we were conceived, who created the church and brought us into it to make something, with him, out of this still incomplete, unfinished world.

I'm not saying we need to return to a manufacturing economy to get what that means or to understand that God is still creating, with us, his creation, bringing it to the day of fulfillment and completion. But I am saying, especially in this consumer driven, self-absorbed age in which we live it's easy to forget we are co-creators with the Creator of life.

Maybe it wouldn't hurt to stop every now and then and stand in front of our Creation window—at the east end on the north wall of this sanctuary—and remind ourselves, as the stained-glass artist so magnificently does, that God didn't just bring everything into being and then walk away. Rather God is here, hovering over the troubled waters of the world like an artist contemplating how to shape you and me and this planet into the masterpiece he envisions. Amen.

– All Saints Sunday –

Heaven
Hebrews 9:11-14

November 1, 2015

On All Saints Sunday, I think of Dante Alighieri the great Italian poet who, in his *Divine Comedy*, gave the world the best sermon ever preached on heaven. Dante's epic takes him from his 14th century Tuscan world to the tenth sphere of heaven where the saints reside for eternity in the presence of God. His reader is ushered through the darkest regions of Hell to the shifting light of Purgatory and finally into the Empyrean bliss. For Dante, the highest sphere of heaven lay like an outermost skin over the physical world. And while we live in an age of black holes and Hubble telescopes that make his ascending spheres of heaven seem ordinary, his age had a greater capacity for mystery and likely elicited a deeper sense of wonder and awe at the magnificence of the created order.

I start with a poet to talk about heaven because theologians are more concerned with doctrinal infrastructure but artists like Dante and Dan Forrest, composer of today's Requiem, bring color and imagination to the possibilities of afterlife. Our national poet laureate Charles Wright, for example, raises an interesting question about how to find heaven. In his *Zone Journal* poems, he remembers the birth and death dates of his muses—Paul Cezanne, John Keats, and Ezra Pound—and in a poem titled, "A Traveler between life and death" Wright wonders where do we draw the line between this world and the next? Where do they meet? Where is the synapse between mortality and eternity? The common ground, where one gives way to the other?

His answer is that heaven is to be found where "That line like a wind over water/Rippling toward shore,/appears and disappears/In wind-rise and wind-falter–/That line between rain and sleet,/between leaf-bronze and leaf-drop–/That line where the river stops and the sea begins,/Where the black blackens/and light comes out of light..."

Dan Forrest asks the same question in his choral work today and, like Wright, he blurs the line, suggesting perhaps a dotted line separating this world and the next. The title of his work says as much: "Requiem for the Living"; in five movements he takes us from the struggles and joys of this life–and joins them to the saints in heaven who know a life more full and complete than ours.

All great art is the old made new; the idea of merging of earth and heaven, a dotted line between, goes back to Augustine and continues through Aquinas, Calvin, and Edwards. What fascinated them was the continuation of relationships in this world to the next. Mark Twain even gets into the act saying in *Huckleberry Finn* that surely if there is a heaven it must be a bigger one than that of Huck's Aunt, Mrs. Phelps, whose view of the afterlife was no more than "a mean little ten-cent heaven about the size of Rhode Island."

While as many as 81% of us, according to a recent poll, believe in some form of life after death, we spend precious little time talking about it in church—or more specifically, preachers spend very few words on the subject. When asked about it most people are circumspect and content with, "I haven't the foggiest idea." This is unfortunate because given the porous nature of reality—the reality we can see and the reality we otherwise receive glimpses of or voices from or summons to of one kind or another—given the robust interconnection between this world and the one that is our final destination, it makes good sense to contemplate, at least once each year, a created order bigger than our senses can perceive or a powerful telescope in low-earth orbit can measure.

The benefit of days such as this, remembering the trajectory of creation, is that it allows us to realign our operating view of life with the biblical vision; to connect the dots of human existence with the fullness of God's purposes, and thus live with deeper expectation and awe and confidence.

Paul Tillich said the categories we use to talk about such things are not measurable by time and space; yet it does make sense, he agrees, to talk of heaven in earthly terms, if we remember our metaphors are placeholders for something much greater. The reason Dante's heaven is revered above all others is the synthesis he makes of a God-centered afterlife set in terms of human community.

Marilynne Robinson's preacher in *Gilead* did the same thing; he said heaven is a world much like this one only twice as good; "I'd multiply by ten or twelve and not just two," he says from his deathbed to his old confidant "but two is much more sufficient for my purposes." His friend looks at him, pleased, "sitting there multiplying the feel of the wind by two, the smell of the grass by two, the practical jokes he played as a boy.... the stars were brighter in those days," the dying man says. "Twice as bright," his friend replies.

We are, on our best days, in our best moments, living the life of heaven, the life our loved ones we name today are living every moment of every immeasurable era of eternity. It is this principle of the fullness of life the *Westminster Confession* has in mind when it says, "The chief end of humans is to serve God and *enjoy Him forever.*"

What you will hear from Sawrie Becker in a moment is a story that recognizes a larger reality, a bigger world than the one we can see and touch; it is a world where life is stronger than death and love never dies. Most of us could tell that story. Just two weeks ago when Carol and I went to Cincinnati to perform the graveside service for our niece's four-month old son, our grandnephew; *you* were with us; we felt *your prayers, your loving embrace* and we were able to affirm again that life does not end with death. So let the music blur the line for you today between here and there; let the story Sawrie tells merge the best of this world with the world to come; and let your actions, every one of them, be a sign of gratitude for the living God who stands by us in this life and welcomes us home when our days here are ended. Amen.

– Christ The King –

Judged
Matthew 25:31-46

November 23, 2014

It's been quite a week, starting with more disturbing news from ISIS and the execution of an American citizen. In Israel, an extremist attack on a Jewish prayer service resulted in five deaths. Thursday night, the President made a brave and compelling case for the temporary relief of five million people who live under the specter of deportation. Then, joining the record books of surprise storms in WNY a week-long lake effect event pummeled the region, taking twelve lives and disrupting tens of thousands of others. Not to mention ongoing reports of the Ebola crisis.

Perhaps it's human to search for some meaning or reason in the wake of such events. If we can answer the question "why did these things happen?" we can gain a sense of control over our lives and keep chaos at bay.

This morning's story doesn't explain why the week unfolded as it did, but it does offer a perspective that helps make some sense of it. The parable leaps forward to the end of time, which enables us to look back, as it were, with the clarity of hindsight. Matthew wants us to see our present circumstances by stepping out of them to gain a more compelling perspective and a way we might respond to them.

Interestingly, the parable is referred to as the "Judgment of the Nations," which suggests it is a fitting lens through which to look at the world stage. This is the last of three parables we've considered over the past three Sundays. The stories grab our attention because of the anticipated final accounting. The idea of a final judgment reminds us, in case we've forgotten, and reaffirms for us, in case we're in doubt, that we live in a universe where actions of right and wrong have eternal consequences.

Matthew uses these stories for a church in danger of losing sight of its relevance and disengaging from the world. The long wait for Jesus' second coming had atrophied the sinews of social justice in the Jerusalem church. This assessment of a congregation is not uncommon. Mission and outreach are constantly evolving; churches must discern where God is calling them.

Finding such purpose requires keeping a pulse on the community where there is need and an eye on the congregation where there are human and material resources and in what way they might be reasonably and bravely connected.

The first Christian communities were experiments in pure communism—living together, sharing possessions, welcoming those in need, reaching out to those isolated by social custom or legal restriction.

I can't imagine those things ever "just happened" by themselves. It required leadership, communication and organizational skill, but more than that the success of the early church depended upon what St. Paul refers to in his letter to the church in Galatia as the fruits of the spirit—love, joy, peace, patience, kindness, generosity, faithfulness, gentleness, and self-control.

I remember years ago thinking that life in a monastery would be easy compared with life in the real world, but my monastic friend laughed and said, "We suffer, too, from inflated egos and greed as much as the outside world; it's just more obvious in here. We're all human." Being and living in Christian community may not require complex systems and organizational charts as much as it does principles and behavior that results in simple acts of kindness and caring as Mother Theresa said— which is the point of today's parable, particularly if we read it in the context of the life of the early church to whom it was addressed.

I wonder sometimes if the promise of Jesus's imminent return didn't shift, at some point, say toward the end of the second generation after Jesus, from being an expected reality to a good excuse for the church to 'keep watch' and ignore the challenges of facing the world, to the hard task of becoming a functional mission organization. We see it today. Many churches fall into a deadly survivalist self-satisfaction that revolves around maintenance of the building and fiscal responsibility—important as they are, hardly reasons for a church to exist.

Whereas, for congregations engaged in mission, building and fiscal matters are lower on the list of priorities while mission is on top; consequently, they find themselves engaged in a creative mix of innovation, entrepreneurial skill, teamwork and flexibility. Such communities have an energy that is infectious and palpable.

Let me get back to the parable. Matthew's story of the Judgment of the Nations is a lens to consider some of the events of the past week. I don't mean to suggest that it is a crystal ball or one-size-fits-all answer for the struggles of the human family. But it does give us a helpful benchmark or plumb line of human compassion that might be a guide when we live through a crisis-filled week like the one we just had.

It is telling that neither the sheep nor the goats have any idea it is Jesus they are ministering to, or not, as is the case. Kind of like the time a Swedish newspaper reporter telephoned Sinclair Lewis to tell him that he had won the Nobel Prize in literature. Lewis thought it was a practical joke and began to imitate the man's accent. But it was not a joke: Lewis was, in fact, the first American to win the Nobel Prize in literature. "When did we see thee, hungry, thirsty, a stranger, naked or in prison," they ask. To which the Son of Man proclaims, "Inasmuch as you did it to one of the least of these you did it to me." Christ identifies himself, unequivocally, with those in need. It is Christ himself we serve when we serve them.

Not only are those who act in compassion acting in compassion toward a fellow human being, they are acting in compassion to the Creator and Giver of life; and, those who do not show compassion end up disregarding the source of life and blessing for what can only be, reading between the lines of this parable, self-serving, self-absorbed reasons.

Each human is a child of God, of ultimate value and worth; honoring the sacred gift of life by caring for those who are broken is what ultimately matters. We may go through the motions of being faithful church members and responsible citizens, but if we do not respond where there is suffering, the rest is of little importance in the present and of no consequence eternally. St. Paul said the same thing to the Corinthians, "If I have not love I am a noisy gong and clanging cymbal. Even though I possess great gifts and accomplish many things, if I have not love I gain nothing."

About the extremist acts of the past week, it doesn't take this or any parable to condemn those acts. Which is not to say that mere condemnation will provide a more peaceful world. The rise of an organization like ISIS that claims to have established a Muslim caliphate or kingdom is the result of a complex set of circumstances. Its appeal to young men around the world depends upon a profound sense of ethnic and economic disenfranchisement that has accumulated over generations. The attack by two Palestinian Muslims on a Jewish prayer service is also the result of long-standing disenfranchisement and more recent rejection of Palestinian hopes for sovereignty. Years of failure to negotiate self-determination lie beneath the Palestinian rage.

The parable raises the question of who is hungry, thirsty, a stranger, sick, naked and imprisoned in the case of Middle East turmoil. A good answer might be: everyone—Jews, Muslims, citizens, even extremists. Perhaps a more difficult question than who is in need in the Middle East is how do we respond to those in need–on all sides of all of the conflicts? If I knew the answer to that question I would be in Tehran preparing for the final day of nuclear talks tomorrow. Though I am not sure anyone there has the answer either.

But I was a part of a group of Presbyterian leaders who placed an ad in the NY Times on Thursday this past week (and which is now posted on our website). The statement calls for, among other things, the church's biblical role as a 'repairer of the breach,' working with people of all faith traditions. The extremists on either side of every conflict from Israel to Syria to the U.S. Congress are dominating the conversation and winning the day.

It is time to claim a bold voice and create a moderate middle ground where we can have conversation, find compromise and negotiate real solutions. The centrifugal forces at work in society that are moving away from the center are formidable. They claim to be normative and they use, with unctuous piety, platitudes of patriotic and religious purity to justify their destructive ends. It will take bold, persistent and clear-visioned leadership to reconstruct a coherent, peaceful public square where diversity is welcomed and celebrated.

Some of you would prefer I not bring politics into a sermon but I don't see how not to talk about the President's action Thursday night, especially with today's text admonishing us to welcome the stranger. The President is not perfect. There are things he might have done differently or better or not at all. But the decision to lift, temporarily, the specter of fear for five million people trapped in a lethal catch-22–people whom we are content to let clean our motel rooms and landscape our homes, yet whom we subject to interrogation and deportation at any minute if they are stopped by the authorities; and not just deportation but separation from their spouses and children. Thus, they live in daily fear of losing their loved ones. Can you imagine leaving the house tomorrow morning with that hanging over your head or the heads of your children? The President did the right thing.

The fact that we would tolerate this in the United States of America is unconscionable. I am afraid we have tolerated it because of the not so hidden agenda of more than a few politicians and their billionaire backers. The clear and stated goal of these self-identified patriots is to discredit, defeat and destroy nearly anything with the name Obama on it.

And so we have descended into a status quo of chaos sustained by the incessant, press conference drumbeat of fear including sequesters, random deportations, gerrymandered voting districts, outlandish requirements to exercise the sacred right to vote, new threats of a government shut-down, repeal of health care for eight million people who previously fell between the cracks, and refusal to approve a backlog of judicial appointments that has nearly paralyzed the federal courts.

The parable tells us that acts of kindness trump all other human activities, including any reasons or excuses to avoid or null or discredit such acts. What matters is that a human life has been helped, and in so being helped the very life of God in us and in the human family is nurtured and strengthened.

From the perspective of the end of time, Republican and Democrat agendas and the internecine battles waged between them will not even register on the eternal scales of justice and mercy, but the failure to act with compassion which is precisely what those battles are about will weigh heavily for those who abdicated their responsibility as elected officials and worshipped instead the god of money, power and re-election. Their accountability and just reward will be meted out in the kingdom of heaven; just as it will for each of us, according to the extent to which we did or did not show mercy and compassion to the least of these. Amen.

Occasions and Themes in the Life of a Congregation

– Abundance V. Scarcity –

The First Miracle
John 2:1-11

January 17, 2016

I have enlightening conversations with my barber, who is really a hair stylist–there is a difference of course–but that's another matter. Gabe, my hair stylist, is a wealth of information–perhaps a trait common to the profession. He happens to be a lifelong student of music, movies and sit-coms, and he's something of a foodie. Last Thursday, Gabe was telling me about a documentary he watched recently on the famous debate in 1968 between Gore Vidal and William F. Buckley. It may have been the first point/counter point programming for television; little did they know in 1968 the Pandora's Box of political punditry and protest that would open and spew forth in the years to come.

Gabe's point, other than telling me how Vidal got under Buckley's skin, provoking him to make unsavory comments which gave Vidal the win, Gabe's point was the high level of discourse and vocabulary the liberal and conservative icons employed. Compared to the political discourse we hear today, he said, it was vastly more nuanced and complex, not to mention their vocabulary—big words we don't hear in the media today. Some of you in higher education have said writing and general knowledge skills have dropped; and while funding and support for science and technology has increased, the arts and humanities have been cut back or eliminated. Marketable, vocational skills have replaced classic education that taught people how to think.

David Brooks says our age is "beauty-poor and meaning-deprived." [i] Growing illiteracy is entertaining on late night TV when people are asked about the Bible or American history; but it is cause for concern when we hear of the appeal of political candidates with simplistic answers for complex issues that are little more than sound bites aimed to rouse fear and anger.

As far back as Alexis de Tocqueville, reducing things to simplistic terms was a noticeable trend. He said there were, in his time, those who, "in the name of progress, seek to reduce man to a material being. They look for what is useful without concern for what is just; they seek science removed from faith and prosperity apart from virtue. They style themselves as champions of modern civilization." [ii]

Maybe it all goes back to the Enlightenment when science in its rebellious adolescence rejected the legitimacy of subjective knowledge and experience. The point I want to make is that it would be easy, in our modern secular age, even in a church, to dismiss the miracle at Cana simply because it is called a miracle; then there is the apparent non-point of it, unlike his other miracles when people were healed or fed; plus Jesus' brusque comment to his mother, and her strange instruction to the servants to do whatever he told them.

Given these 'loose ends' I want to avoid our falling either into the trap of explaining the miracle away by seeing it only as a story with symbolic meaning or into the other trap of trying to explain something that is, 2000 years later to our 21st century eyes, inexplicable. Maybe you're thinking that doesn't leave much room to find the redeeming value of this story. But I ask your patience and consideration.

If the miracle is not about symbols and can't be explained what is it about? The late Rev. Dr. Peter Gomes, Chaplain of Harvard University, says, "It is the *shortage* which provides the context for the manifestation of the wine. We used to say the age of miracles was past. We perform modern miracles at Raytheon and General Motors. Miracles are ordered up on a daily and scientific basis at Massachusetts General Hospital and explained at M.I.T." [iii]

But what Gomes suggests to his Harvard audience is that the miracle at Cana is a story about God's unexpected abundance in the midst of scarcity. For those early believers the world was increasingly limiting and narrow. They were being rejected and ejected from their homes and synagogues. The state was making life as a Christian harder to sustain. Jesus' turning the water into wine took place in the context of not having enough, of shortage, of life-threatening scarcity.

Which provides our connection to this ancient text. In a world that pretends to be fact-based, logic-driven and superstition-free, a world in which technology has given us so much, in a nation *that has* so much, what could we possibly be lacking? Dr. Gomes offers an answer; he says we have a shortage of what he calls the "vital elements of life," including our spirit; living without these vital elements is becoming a way of life in the US. Is it possible, he asks, that what we have is not what we need, and our state of need begins with civility and branches in many related directions that include our mental and physical health and social and economic well-being?

114

Gomes claims we are in a very real sense a 'have not' nation. We might at least acknowledge, he says, that things aren't as they once were; not to play the game of "Ain't it awful' or sell the illusion that some golden age, which may have never existed, is now long past. But to find common ground with those for whom this story was first intended. Maybe it is enough to say, as the President did last week, it's time to stop shooting ourselves in the foot, to fix our politics and move into the future. But it is hard to imagine how that will happen without being honest about the shortage of those "vital elements of life" across the nation, in this community, perhaps in our own lives.

The miracle at Cana is about much more than the singular act of turning water into wine. It is a story that announces that God will be present through this Jesus to people in need; it is in our weakness and dependence, not our strength, that God can do wondrous things with and for us. Who would have thought America is a needy nation? Or the Presbyterian Church a needy church? We were taught things of their nature get better and to every problem there is a solution, that prosperity with its accompanying technology is just around the corner; and to recite the mantra of bigger and better every year. Yet, to come of age is to confront one's needs, to come up short, to recognize we are lacking, if not technology and material things, then human connections.

Every miracle Jesus performed was in response to an acknowledged need or lack or scarcity. Transformation is the name of his enterprise and ministry. The Jesus of the Gospel of John is like the birthday candle you can't blow out. He keeps showing up, taking the initiative, confronting poverty and disease, despair and failure, and transforms the people held back and paralyzed by fear. He is the Source of Life itself; he finds himself surrounded by rigid religion, an atheist state and unjust social practices and conditions. The people clamor to touch him, to have him touch them, to be relieved of their lameness or disease or blindness; to be saved from death.

Unlike the Jesus of Matthew, Mark and Luke, John's Jesus appears to read people's minds, to be in two places at once and to be unencumbered by traditional expectations for who a messiah should be and what he should do. When Jesus arrives reality is exploded, cracked open. At the well where he meets a woman of ill-repute, at the pool of Bethsaida where a lame man waits for the waters to stir, and along the road where a leprous man shunned by the community calls out to him. Finally, he comes to his friend Lazarus' home, apparently too late after Lazarus has died, and Jesus calls the dead man to walk from his tomb. Miracles yes, not to prove or disprove, but to accept

115

or not as God's relentless search for the lost, God's unconditional offer of new and abundant life.

This is the weekend on which we remember The Reverend Dr. Martin Luther King, Jr. In many ways significant progress has been made in race relations and socio-economic equity, but it seems the more forward momentum we gain—electing a black President for example—the more behind we realize we are—the wave of police shootings of unarmed, innocent black men and boys over the past year. Or maybe you find yourself in some untenable circumstance of health or home or career. Perhaps your resources of spirit and resilience have ebbed and there's nothing left; you've come up short; you're in some rigid reality that offers no relief, no promise of changing or getting better.

What's a nation with ongoing racial injustice, what's a person with depleted personal resources of mind, body and spirit, what's a church in a society of growing anti-religious sentiment and secular rejection of mystery and wonder to do? John says there was a wedding in Cana in Galilee that ran out of wine. Jesus showed up and gave them more and better wine than they could have imagined or hoped for.

If it's the word "miracle" that hangs you up, then try using the word "grace." And then as you face a new week in a new year with the same old challenges and intractable worries or anxiety or problems, simply recite the words of the ancient liturgy, "Come, Lord Jesus, come." Then prepare yourself for the intervention of God's abundance. Amen.

i. David Brooks, "When Beauty Strikes," *NYTimes*, Saturday, 1/16/16, A27.
ii. Marilynne Robinson, *The Givenness of Things*, (Farrar, Straus, Giroux, New York: 2015) 75.
iii. William Willimon, *Pulpit Resource*, January to March 2016, 16.

– Beauty –

Gratitude in Every Action: Worship, Music and The Arts
Mark 10:17-31

October 18, 2015

There's a painting in the Metropolitan Museum of Art, on the second floor, in the gallery where the works of the Hudson River School are kept. The painting is of an Adirondack trout pond, secluded and still, somewhere deep in the woods. When I stand before that painting the calm and peace of it descend over me; my racing mind begins to slow and let go of the orbiting obligations and burdens big and small. My heart comes to a contented watchful, openness. Landscape, said the Chinese poet Weng Wei, smooths the rough edges of the soul.

This is our first "Gratitude in Action" Sunday. We celebrate and give thanks today for the role beauty plays in our lives as people of faith. Specifically, I want to lift up the inseparable connection between beauty–music and art specifically this morning–in the life of God's people in general and in our worship life in particular. Hard as it is to believe, there is a long and studied ambivalence toward art and religious faith in the Christian tradition. While the church has been from its earliest beginning a patron of the arts, there is another side of our history starting with Augustine, echoed in Aquinas, and reinforced during the Reformation, that looked with skepticism on any role for music and art in the life of the church.

Aquinas, for example, said preachers and teachers should not be involved in singing lest they neglect "greater things." During the Reformation, many towns and villages witnessed the destruction of church art by zealous Reformers who interpreted literally the injunction of Torah that "thou shalt have no other gods before me or make graven images of me." It was not a proud moment in our history; rather than a righteous faith, such destruction reveals a deep fear that beauty will displace God, that it will become an idol, and that religion will be reduced to what merely brings pleasure to the senses.

Tom Troeger of Yale Divinity School says that even those who have widened their concept of beauty to include moral and spiritual beauty often fail to relate these to natural and artistic beauty. They tend to depreciate the latter–

117

the beauty of the earth and works of art created by human hands and minds—rather than see these tangible forms as a means for the expression, nurture, and deepening of faith. But there is another vision of the role beauty plays in the life of faith and the ministry of the church. It is a counter-cultural vision, a prophetic vision that speaks to the image of God within us and our innate ability to recognize what is true and right and good.

Through music and art—and I pause here to acknowledge the wealth of both that we are privileged to enjoy and sustain here at Westminster—from the glory of this room and building and campus to our historic and current excellence of music ministry—through music and art we are drawn to what is good and true in a world filled with terrors and injustice. Without beauty the life of faith becomes grim and onerous; we distort the image of God within us and in our understanding of God's character, concentrating on God's power and might and missing the plethora of divine attributes that enhance and sustain the human experience.

An unimaginative and artistically starved faith diminishes both God and us. The great preacher Fred Craddock said, "Extract from a person's life a healthy portion of songs and flowers and you have reduced to something less than human 'the creature the Lord God has made to have dominion over land and sea.'" [i] In a society that commercializes beauty and sells it as 'the beautiful life' intended for a privileged social and economic elite who think of beauty as being young, fit, rich and glamorous—true beauty embodied in music and art contradicts the inhuman and provides alternative visions to those that oppress. Beauty redeems. Art does not simply mirror reality; it challenges reality's destructive and alienating tendencies.

Today's Gospel tells of a rich, young ruler. He is a man whose heart is starved and whose life is enslaved. His capacity to present a 'successful' image—"all these things I have done from my youth"—is the goal of his every waking moment, conforming as he does to outward appearance and expectations and discounting the voice inside, the voice that knows he is unhappy and longs for true joy. Jesus sees through the man and loves him, Mark says. He does not wish to expose or judge the man, only to offer him the path of life. And just as rescue workers seek to get the gun out of the hand of a suicidal person, Jesus tells the man to let go of that which is killing him—his possessions which, sadly, the man is unable to do because, Mark says, he had many possessions.

This story reveals the tension between the possession of material things and faith; the rich young ruler has lived a rule-based vs. a principle-guided life; his faith has been reduced to a formula for passing what he thinks is life's religious test to get to some promised land of worry-free comfort and happiness. Sadly, the man's soul has not been awakened by beauty; the image of God within him has been starved by his pursuit of material things; a recent article on the workplace observed that financial reward does not tap into the essence of human motivation so much as rewire it. When money is made the measure of all things, it becomes the measure of all things—a self-justifying, self-fulfilling philosophy that leads to despair and loneliness.

But we are more complicated creatures; there is something within us—call it the image of God or the intrinsic power of life—that recognizes and realizes what we are made for; that understands the innate oneness of life; that we find our true joy in connection with one another, with God and with all living things; and that knows there is nothing in this life, no disgrace or calamity, as one writer said, that God and nature cannot repair. The power and beauty of life does not reside in nature or humans alone but in the harmony of both.

Little wonder then that music and art return us to ourselves. Harmony of colors in painting or movement in dance or sound in music embody and point to the deep harmony we find when we give ourselves away; when we treat the neighbor as we would ourselves, when the last become first and the first, last. Is it any wonder that the stained glass in this room, the blended earth colors of the walls, the sublime music that wafts over us from the choir loft take us to a place where words alone struggle to reach?

I was speaking with a wise, retired pastor of this presbytery recently and, she said, "I have always believed that after a minister the second person a church must hire is not an educator or youth worker but a musician because music is transcendent and feeds the soul of the congregation. A good sermon," she said, "might be partly transcendent, but music consistently lifts us into the realm of the holy, the realm of eternal life."

Friends, we have much to be thankful for today—a robust ministry of worship, music and the arts. It is strange how we can take even these remarkable gifts for granted. I remember one of the first Sundays I sat in this chancel seventeen years ago; the reader had to elbow me because it was my turn to lead worship, yet I had become so enraptured by the windows, especially the ethereal blue, that I was just sitting, blissfully staring at them while the congregation waited for the order of worship to proceed.

Now I can walk through this sanctuary on a busy day and barely notice them. We dare not take the beauty that surrounds us in this sanctuary for granted; let us relish and embrace the soaring chorus, the strong hymns, the silence, the prayers and all that points to the innate oneness of life. It is a oneness too

119

often obscured in a world where wealth is highly cherished while our neighbor, too often, lies hungry and sick, like Lazarus, at the door.

We have work to do–a new world to bring into being. If gratitude in action means anything, it means that you and I have the power to embody, to enact, to express not just in our words but in our deeds the oneness of life, the harmony in which God made us and intends all things to flourish. Just as there is harmony in a Bach fugue or African American spiritual so there is harmony when we share from our abundance with a world in want; harmony and beauty when we fall on our knees to praise and thank the Source of Life.

Nothing else, as the rich ruler failed to realize, can feed the inherent and essential hunger of our souls–nothing else makes us at one with the world God made. Amen.

i. Fred Craddock, *As One Without Authority*, (St. Louis: Chalice Press, 1979), 71.

– Leadership –

From Hubris to Humility
2 Samuel 7:1-14a

July 22, 2012

Even though the word covenant is not used, that is what today's story from Second Samuel is about–it is about making a new covenant with the Davidic kingdom for the future of Israel. In other words, this story, like Genesis 8 when God makes a promise to Noah never to destroy life on earth again, and Genesis 12 when God calls Abraham and Sarah to a new land and promises to bless and multiply their family, and Exodus 20 when God gives Moses and the people a new law for living in the wilderness and promises to lead them to a land of milk and honey, today's story from 2 Samuel recounts another watershed moment in Israel's history. God selects David to be the representative for the nation. From now on David's dynasty is the means by which Yahweh will govern Israel, and all who defy this dynasty will be considered rebels and apostates.

2 Samuel 7 is a pivotal text; much hinges on this story of fidelity between the king and Yahweh. Another key player, the prophet Nathan, is also introduced. He is presented as not just a trusted advisor to the king, but first and foremost a reliable communicator of God's will. It is Nathan later who calls a spade a spade and levels the sentence against David for his adulterous relationship with Bathsheba. In many ways, Nathan, not David, is the benchmark for fidelity to Yahweh, although God depends on a true and trusted relationship with the king in order to continue to shape Israel's destiny.

Flawed as David as, Yahweh chose him still–at least that is the message of the story today–and this was an important message to communicate in a time when the northern and southern kingdoms were divided. Tribal leaders vied for the honor of being God's chosen monarch to lead Israel from nomadic life to national prominence. This is the context for David's deciding to build Yahweh a house and Yahweh's instead choosing to remain in the simple temporary housing he has known since the early days of the nomadic wandering.

121

The writer of the story masterfully plays on the Hebrew word for house: bet. The house that David refers to is the national temple or cathedral where God will be worshipped; the *house* God refers to when he says he is building David a house is the dynasty itself-the moral/ethical/political entity that governs and defends Israel.

This is much more than real estate one-upsmanship. It is an inside look at God's chosen leader David—a man who is lulled by the opulence and power he has accumulated into thinking that it is by his own brilliance and strength that Israel is on its way to becoming a great nation, when, in fact, Israel's rising prominence is because of God's decision to bless David's military ventures. The fate of Israel, the story implies, will turn on fidelity to God and God's mission for the nation. The dispute over who will build whom a house signals that David's hubris is getting in the way of his being the effective leader God needs him to be.

What we have here then from 2 Samuel is a very old story about the ongoing challenges and pitfalls of leadership. Just a week ago the *New York Times* ran an interesting article entitled, "The Spreading Scourge of Corporate Corruption." Big banks in the U.S. and Britain have violated the most basic principle upon which capitalist economy is based: trust. The parade of business leaders accused of misdeeds, booted from the executive suite and even occasionally jailed, is undermining this essential tenet upon which our society rests. The article goes on to say that bigger markets allow bigger frauds. Bigger companies, with more complex balance sheets, have more places to hide fraud. A twenty-year study indicates that the most lucrative strategy for executives at too-big-to-fail banks would be to loot them to pay themselves vast rewards, knowing full well that the government would save them from bankruptcy.

When trust is the casualty in a complex developed economy, waves of mistrust can spread like an infectious disease. After years of dismal employment prospects, Americans are losing trust in a wide range of institutions, including Congress, the Supreme Court, the presidency, public schools, labor unions and the church. Some tie mistrust to long term unemployment; some lay it at the door of too-big-to-fail corporations; others blame the increasing 'winner take all' economic climate toward which we seem to be hurtling.

But certainly in every case, leadership is at the intersection of the institution, its mission and society at large; and in recent years it appears that leadership in every arena has lost its moral/ethical/spiritual compass. I can give you a

122

very simple, rather ordinary example from the church. An old friend and classmate of mine who was called to one of the nation's most prominent congregations several years ago was dismissed after it was alleged that he was having an affair. From the public accounts of the episode and inadvertently running into a few of the members of that congregation, what it appears to me happened is that my friend who was hugely successful at this prestigious church began to lose his better judgment. Among other things he may have started believing that he was indeed a sort of Midas-touch minister for whom everything he started, blessed or advocated turned to gold. Add to that a driven workaholism and the negative consequences for family life and there was a disaster waiting to happen.

The ordeal cost him his position and forced a period of rehabilitation. He fell from the pinnacle of the church's grace and leadership because he lost touch with his inner compass; you might also say he violated his fidelity to God and God's mission and started making bad decisions. I don't mean to hold my classmate up as an evil person today but merely as a human being; all of us go through periods of losing our way, misplacing our spiritual/moral compass, making poor decisions that disrupt the lives of others. My classmate's example just happens to be somewhat dramatic and, it occurs to me, has more than a little in common with King David.

Leadership is a major issue today as it was for Israel in her prime. As we approach the fall elections we will have an opportunity to select which leadership we want for the next four years. I thought Mayor Michael Bloomberg was right on the other day when he challenged the two men vying to be president to demonstrate moral leadership and make some definitive statements if not proposals about gun control–after yet another horrific mass killing in Colorado.

I can imagine both Governor Romney and President Obama coming up with all sorts of reasons why it is not expedient to tackle the gun control issue at this time–the main reason for which is the power of the gun lobby–but these are just the sort of knotty issues leaders have to deal with. The question today's text raises is what compass does a leader use–his own self-serving goals or a set of higher principles and truths.

The other issue worth putting on the table is the future of liberal or progressive Christianity. This is also a leadership issue. In his latest editorial Ross Douthat asked the question "Can Liberal Christianity Be Saved?" He uses the Episcopal Church as his test case but it could just as easily apply to any mainline denomination including the Presbyterian Church. What

123

Douthat notes is that the more progressive the Episcopal Church becomes the more it shrinks. The hemorrhaging of members over the past decades raises the question of what the church will look like in a few years if things don't change.

Both religious and secular liberals have been loath to recognize this crisis, Douthat says. Leaders of liberal churches have alternated between seeing their decline with a Monty Python-esque "it's just a flesh wound," to an odd and hard to defend self-righteousness about their looming extinction. Few of the outraged critiques of the Vatican's investigation of progressive nuns, for example, mention the fact that Rome is intervening (albeit inappropriately) in part because otherwise the orders in question will likely disappear in a generation. Fewer note the consequences of the eclipse. Douthat says because progressive Catholicism has failed to inspire a new generation of sisters, Catholic hospitals across the nation are passing into the hands of more bottom-line focused administrators with inevitable consequences for how they serve the poor.

The defining idea of progressive Christianity that faith should spur social reform as well as personal conversion has been an immensely positive force in our national life. No one should wish for its extinction; least of all its members. Its leaders stand by while it withers and while Christianity becomes the exclusive property of the political right. What could happen instead is that progressive Christianity might recover a religious reason for its own existence.

The Christianity that inspired causes such as the Social Gospel and the civil rights movement was much more dogmatic than present-day liberal faith. Its leaders and members were deeply grounded in Bible study, family devotions, personal prayer and worship. They argued for both progressive reform and a personal transcendent God, the divinity of Christ, the need of personal redemption and the importance of Christian missions.

Yet by contrast the liberal progressive voice in the church and seminaries today doesn't seem to be offering anything that can't be found in over-the-counter self-help and secular liberalism. Denuding the Bible and Jesus of mystery and divinity makes interesting academic debate but also erodes the natural incubator for faith formation—trust in a higher power.

Leaders in the progressive church, which includes congregations like ours, would do well to consider not only what must be changed about traditional, historic Christianity but also what must be saved. It seems like we're at a crossroads in so many sectors of society. Leadership is key to where we are headed or not headed. And within leadership the question of fidelity to God and God's mission.

These are issues that don't have easy answers but are worthy of our consideration. No generation has faced exactly the issues we face interpreting the faith in the context of a predominantly modern, secular world. One thing is for certain: spiritual hunger is common to every generation and may be more prevalent today than ever. I believe the Christian church, the Presbyterian Church, and Jesus Christ have much to offer our hurting, war-torn, corruption-riddled world.

Let's keep the conversation on leadership going and figure out what David struggled to figure out: how to maintain fidelity to God in our personal spiritual practice and discern where we are being led on the issues of the day. Amen.

– Progressives and Evangelicals –

When God Rolls Up Her Sleeves: Base of Operations
Matthew 4:12-23

January 26, 2014

We've been talking about Jesus and the movement that sprang up, followed him and grew in his wake as he began preaching in Galilee. From his birth to his baptism to his three years of teaching and healing the stars were aligned, the timing just right for his appearance on the stage of world history. But it wasn't just timing and stars. His movement became known as "The Way"– the name for the practice of the principles he taught. Before people were known as Christians, they were known as followers of The Way. I like that designation because it implies movement, a path, action toward life; it evokes, as the word "Christian" does not, something pragmatic, hands-on, and living.

Yet, it wasn't just the practice of principles that captivated the hearts of his followers and turned the world upside down–as it is still turning the world upside down from Buffalo to Beijing. You might say we are dealing with two religions: the "religion of Jesus"–what he said and did–and the "religion about Jesus", what was concluded about him, his ministry and his teaching. We are, by definition, participants in that second order of access to Jesus' life. We are those he referred to when he revealed his wounds to Thomas and said, "Blessed are those who have not seen and yet believe."

And here is one of the distinguishing features of Christian faith. As limited as our access to the historical Jesus is, given the boundaries of space and time and a very fragmented collection of texts and historical materials, Christians still claim that Jesus meets us as powerfully and personally as those whom he first called. If we can encounter Jesus the person in our present circumstances, then we too can experience his life-transforming message and join the ranks of that first generation; this claim is unique among followers of the world's religions. "I will not leave you orphaned," Jesus said at the Last Supper. "I am coming to you. In a little while the world will not see me. But you will see me. Because I live, you also will live."

126

It is the living presence of Christ, in large measure, that accounts for the explosive growth of the evangelical church, the vitality of the black church and the extraordinary mission and discipline of monastic orders like the Benedictines and Franciscans. The church is our base of operations. But church is more than buildings and traditions and even the bonds of the community. It is a common experience, a common encounter with and commitment to the living presence of Christ.

Soren Kierkegaard emphasized this personal relationship to Jesus in his comparison of Socrates and Jesus as teachers. For Socrates Truth was self-actualization, improving who we are. Once the student learned the Socratic method, that student could find answers to life and fulfillment without the teacher. Yet Jesus is concerned not with merely "improving" permanently flawed creatures but *transforming us* by conveying God's unconditional love despite our flaws. The student never becomes independent of the teacher but increasingly in need of his love and forgiveness.

I want to consider this personal, relational dimension of our faith this morning for a couple of reasons. It's easy to come here and stay in the realm of ideas; plus we live in an increasingly 'virtual' world that lacks what is tangible and real. Like an MP3 player that "shrinks" music digitally; it sounds like the real thing until you hear it in a concert hall. But there's a problem inherent in a cerebral faith or spirituality constructed on thoughts or metaphors alone: it doesn't go with us when we go out the door. To be more exact, it doesn't go with us when we run up against a crisis from a health diagnosis to a career detour to a train wreck in some relationship.

I am not suggesting we abandon intellectual rigor or the exercise of imagination, creativity and problem-solving. But I am saying that the Mainline Church, by and large, has excised the possibility of a personal relationship with God and—more to the point of this morning's story—a personal relationship with Jesus.

Most of us are willing to say, 'Give me Jesus as a moral model or excellent example–but Jesus, a living presence in my life? Not so much!' Yet, when Simon and Andrew put down their fishing nets and came to the voice and call of a man who said "follow me and I will make you fishers of people," they were not responding to an intellectual system or theology or even a worthy role model; they were responding to a human face and voice, a living human presence. This synapse or "meeting" is the spiritual DNA of the church. It can happen anywhere. Thus, our "base of operations" is anywhere we meet and follow Christ. And not just follow but surrender to him as Simon and Andrew surely did.

I would wager there is a direct correlation between the extent to which Jesus is for us a living presence whom we know and understand and trust and the extent to which we are willing to surrender our lives to his call and sovereignty. That is the take away from this brief description of his encounter with those fishermen in Galilee. We're talking first century fishing village culture; we're talking duty to parents; a livelihood passed from one generation to the next; expectations for adult children and sons especially. That these men would simply leave behind, almost without closing the door, their business of fishing, not to mention all of the hardware that went with it, and their father in the boat, to follow this stranger is the punch line of the story.

These are not college graduates taking a year off before business school; nor are they trying to build their resumes by working as interns for a rising political leader. Almost immediately we want to know more. As good higher critics of the Bible we apply the tools of scientific research to the circumstances of the fishermen, expecting to find some rational explanation for their bold decision. But if we do not come back to the original story, to that human moment of meeting and deciding, which even the best of scientific method and tools can never fully uncover, then all we have done is use the story like a piñata, or better, a bull charging straight for our comfortable and settled opinions; so we place our banderillas or spikes into the neck of this vital story, draining the life out of it with each historical "explanation" so that we can destroy its power and claim upon our own lives.

Matthew simply says, "He saw two brothers casting a net into the sea and he said, 'follow me and I will make you fish for people.' *Immediately* they left their nets and followed him." What's a good, Mainline Protestant critic of the Bible to do? This is the fork in the road between us and the evangelical wing of our own church, not to mention a huge portion of those who call themselves Christian in the nation and world. I wonder if there might be some other road, less traveled by either of us, a road that would bring together the paths of intellectual rigor but also personal relationship to and experience of a living Christ both of which were at the heart of our Mother Church, the Church of Scotland from which we emigrated to this nation.

This road split in two directions at the end of the Nineteenth century when our evangelical ancestors (who were, by the way, the prophetic voice that drove abolition of slavery and the spirit of the brave missionaries who took agricultural, medical and educational outreach around the world) the road split when these evangelical ancestors rejected the tools of higher criticism and science and embraced the defense of a more literal interpretation of the Bible; and we in the doctrinal wing of the church exchanged our rigid theology for progressive political views but retained our cold and stiff liturgical forms.

Like sibling rivals we have been unkind to one another; and yet we are members of the same family. Is it possible for us to live under the same roof ever again? The reward would be a richer, deeper, more textured faith for you and me, the Mainline wing; and a more substantive, theologically grounded faith for those on the evangelical side of the family. Of course, these labels fail when we meet real people in either camp, but there is truth to the effects of the split between us and the mutual impoverishment it causes—a split fueled by distrust that leads us often to caricature and label one another.

As the new Pope is advocating for the Roman church, it is time for a new day; it is time for healing and recovery; and perhaps someday a family reunion. What more pressing mission could the church have in our war-torn, violent world but for itself to be an outpost of civility, harmony, mutual respect and dignity for all people? It is fitting that today's story would lead us to such a conclusion. Jesus' move north to Capernaum in Galilee after his baptism in the Jordan, outside of Jerusalem, fulfills the words of the prophet Isaiah who rejoiced that the "people who lived in darkness have seen a great light." These people of Zebulun and Naphtali Isaiah names were not Jews; they lived outside the tight circle of the Jewish law and community. Yet, the Messiah who comes to save, comes to save all of God's children.

This tiny Jewish tradition as far back as the prophet Isaiah envisions not salvation for itself alone, but in keeping with God's charge to Abraham and Sarah 'blessed to be a blessing to all the families of the earth,' anticipates salvation for all. Galilee is the region of gentiles, land of Samaritans and Roman soldiers, bordering other tribes, cults and cultures. That Jesus begins his ministry here is confirmation of his role as the Messiah Isaiah foresaw. At the heart of today's stories is the promise of healing among the tribes and clans and therefore hope and peace as the world never before experienced.

But let's not forget where we started, the encounter with Jesus that impelled those fishermen to leave their nets, their father in the boat, their families and village. Whatever he said (and I think we can take Matthew pretty much at his word that his invitation was to follow him and become fishers of men and women) it struck instantly and deeply in their hearts.

Could it be that whatever he meant had the sound of something so radically new and needed, so refreshingly encompassing and inclusive that when they saw him standing there on the shore and heard his invitation they sensed he had something they and their world had been longing for. Given that he would satisfy a hunger so deep and so wearying my hunch is the choice to respond to him was actually not difficult at all but a choice for life in a world of death. Nor would I be surprised if their choice to follow him was a choice not just for themselves but for their village and families and neighbors *if they could somehow learn to fish for people.*

What we are confronted with today is not so much a question of whether higher criticism of the Bible will permit us to believe this story or explain it to us in a way we can accept. But do we have it in us, *are we willing to trust* a message this big and encompassing so that when we leave the old world we can expect to find his living presence? A message and call encompassing enough that even Jews and gentiles, Mainliners and evangelicals, liberals and conservatives, Republicans and Democrats, gay, straight, bisexual, transgender, black, white, and all the shades in between can find a place together on God's holy mountain. A place of mutual respect and dignity.

If we don't believe that he came with a message that big and meets us personally when we leave our comfortable politically, theologically, economically siloed world behind, then really all we are here for is the slim chance of attracting enough people who look and act and think like us to pay the bills and keep the heat on. Matthew invites us, Jesus *calls us,* to trust and risk for something much more; a call that starts an encounter for us as it did for Simon and Andrew.

An encounter with the living Christ; not just some warmed-over academic description of who a first century Messiah might have been, but a real person, who says, "Because I live, you also will live." A real person, who says let me show you how to share this good news with the world. Amen.

– Suffering –

From Chaos to Understanding
Job 38:1-7

October 11, 2015

Claude didn't read it, but there's a warning from the Theologian General that appears on the title page of the book of Job; it's like the one on tobacco and alcohol products from the Surgeon General. It says: "Warning: the contents of this book can be hazardous to your theological health and spiritual well-being." Everyone who reads Job is at risk; of course, some think that it shouldn't even qualify as sacred text. They say it's really a story about a man who is a pawn in a game between God and Satan; or, that it raises the issue of human suffering and asks all the right questions but doesn't provide any of the right answers; or, that it argues more against than for religious faith.

I've heard all those critiques. I've even argued some of them myself and found them difficult to refute. To be sure, Job is unique; there's no other biblical book quite like it; there are echoes of Job's despair in Ecclesiastes and in the Garden of Gethsemane when Jesus prays for strength and when he feels forsaken on the cross. But no other book is as fully devoted to the subject of human suffering and injustice as Job.

Job is what my playwright friend Neil Wechsler calls a mytho-poetic story—like much great literature of the Western tradition—or Eastern religions and culture. What makes Job unique among epic stories of the ancient Greeks and medieval English and Italians is that it reveals the core identity and beliefs of the Jewish people that become, in part, the core identity and beliefs of Christians.

Here's a deeper analysis from Old Testament scholar Walter Brueggemann: *human utterance* in sacred text is understood as a true and reliable disclosure of who God is. For example, when the psalmist says, "The Lord is my shepherd." But when we consider the utterances of chapter 38 of the Book of Job we notice something very different; we notice that Job's testimony, which is in conflict with Yahweh, leads to a deeper revelation and acceptance of Yahweh. Job's protests and Yahweh's response packaged in a rejection transport them both into a divine/human relationship not found elsewhere in Scripture.

Job and God are on a collision course, but after the wreck they are inseparably linked, having taken the biblical understanding of human suffering out of the realm of morality and justice and into a cosmic perspective bounded by mystery. Scholars have noted how the persistence of the creature, Job, helps to define the Creator, God.

This is a new path to spiritual depth and wholeness; a path that remains undiscovered by many if not most readers of the story who are searching for a more pragmatic and logical explanation for suffering. Of all the utterances about God the biblical writers could have recorded for posterity the councils chose to preserve and remember Job's. Israel's claims for God rely on a fragile human utterance. The Book of Job is a liturgical poem, a lyrical epic, not history, letter, or doctrine. It depicts a universe in which unjustified suffering and an all-powerful God co-exist.

Most of us know the story of Job—he is an upright, honest and faithful man; God says to Satan that Job's faith is so strong that Job will not renounce God for any misfortune that befalls him. Satan accepts the challenge. God then places Job under the dominion of Satan and says he may do with Job what he pleases but not take his life. First come the skin diseases, then the loss of property and family. God does not appear from the time the deal with Satan is struck until the end of the book.

Job petitions God for some explanation, some understanding of his plight. But God is silent, adding to Job's despair. The opening lines of chapter 23 are Job's unvarnished outburst to God, demanding a reason for his suffering. Finally, in today's reading, Yahweh appears but he is lordly, haughty, condescending, dismissive, reprimanding, and refuses to entertain Job's profound question; or to enter into any discussion about justice, sanctions, moral reliability or promises made in Israel's covenant with God. God appears ominously out of a whirlwind; the image by William Blake on the cover of your bulletin is a fair rendering. God speaks. But it is not the ordered, logical, morally balanced voice Job expects. Rather, God is displeased by the temerity of Job's assertions and questions. "Who is this," God thunders, "that darkens counsel by words without knowledge?"

The entire argument Job marshals and relies upon is dead in the water before it begins: the legal argument and model for God; the moral model that faith rewards and sin punishes; the covenant with the Chosen People who are to inherit the earth; the idea that God will be their God and they shall be his people, all previous understandings and theological constructs for the human/divine relationship are null and void.

God announces new ground for his relationship with humans: "Gird up your loins like a man," God says, "I will question you and you will answer me." At this point, most readers of the story check out spiritually if not literally; is this any way to treat an innocent victim? Job, who has been deserted by everyone, is abused by the God to whom he has been ever faithful and devoted.

The ground of God's utterances is the power of a Creator God; this is not the prophets' God of justice. Job and God enter a dialogue for the remainder of the book that depending on how you look at it either leaves the question of suffering egregiously dangling and unanswered or transcends the best categories we must use to deal with our suffering.

The relevance of this book hardly needs to be pointed out; we are surrounded by suffering in virtually all times and places; perhaps it's that we live in a smaller world and are more aware of suffering on the planet than we ever have been. From Syrian refugees to the Black Lives Matter movement; from the re-emergence of oppressive regimes in North Africa and the middle east to victims of fire, earthquake and hurricane most recently in California and the Caribbean to our recent national woes with gun violence, we seem caught in an endless cycle of unjust suffering of the innocent. Then there is our personal suffering, the struggles and troubles of mind and body and spirit we bring to this sanctuary each week.

I've been rereading a little *Moby Dick* recently; one writer says, "The world's grievances are the 'Jobean burden of *Moby Dick*,'" [i] a massive book with a massive theme: the chase of a massive and demonic whale as inseparable from Ahab as God is from Job.

Launched from their New England port with a curse not unlike the one that dooms Job himself, the crew is enflamed with the seething revenge of Captain Ahab, a man possessed; we wonder what compels this crazed mariner when most, having lost a leg to the albino beast, would have called off the hunt long before. Yet, for Ahab as for Job, it is a chase to the finish wherever it may lead, a relentless journey to death and oblivion that cannot be aborted.

The whiteness of the whale, in Melville's words incorporating the very veil of the Christian's Deity on the one hand while on the other, shadowing forth the relentless voids and immensities of the universe, stabs us from behind with the thought of annihilation when beholding the white depths of the Milky Way. This symbol and the story of its pursuit, defiant of rationality and proportion and the measured dictates of reason, is the pursuit Job embarks upon when left for dead by his family and friends. Job wills himself to find and confront God and demand from the Holy One some accounting for the violation of all the principles he lived by and that his suffering represents.

For Ahab and his crew, their chase—like Job's clogged pursuit of answers—leads not to the profitable harvest of a whale or the ordered explanation of his suffering, but to the destruction of the Pequod, her crew and captain just as Job meets the demise of his identity as a man as well as of the God he worshipped. When Yahweh asks Job "where were you when I laid the foundations of the earth; tell me if you have understanding. Who determined its measurements; surely you know!" he invites Job to step back from his human-centered perspective to consider God's unsentimental view of the natural world in which food for the lion's cubs and the eagle's nestlings means the shedding of blood. The radical nature of this book lies in the rejection of Job's model of God as inadequate. Job's categories are too narrow, his conception of God hopelessly human centered. From Job's perspective innocent suffering had to imply the injustice of God. But by the end of the book, Job proclaims, "I have uttered what I did not understand; things too wonderful for me, which I did not know. Hear and I will speak; I will question you and you declare to me. I had heard of you by the hearing of the ear, but now my eyes see you."

Job's sufferings are now seen as part of a vast scheme of creation far too transcendent for any mere mortal to comprehend. Human wisdom is derivative of Yahweh's wisdom and, if there are areas that human wisdom cannot penetrate, it is not because Yahweh's wisdom is deficient. It is because human wisdom is too limited. For all his persistence, Job cannot extricate himself from the limitations of his own humanity.

In the end, Job does not withdraw the questions that obsessed and drove him; it's just that no one is any longer interested in the questions–not Job, not Satan, not God.

This is no longer a God who reneges on his commitments. This is a God in whose presence the issues of moral symmetry and reason are unworthy and trivial.

Rudolf Otto, the great German theologian of comparative religion, had a word for this God–Mysterium Tremendum; the greatest philosopher of the modern era, Immanuel Kant, used such encounters with the holy for his definition of "the Sublime." Charles Darwin, that man who teetered between belief and non-belief, even after losing his oldest beloved child Annie was able to see and say clearly that the wars of nature, famine and death all occur in a larger context that sustains the earth; there is, Darwin said in the last line of the *Origin of Species*, "grandeur in this view of life."

The issue for Job has evolved from "Why do I and other godly people suffer?" to "How may I find peace with this God during my suffering?" Job does not possess the wisdom to contest God. Therefore, he concludes in that final testimony to trust this unfathomable God and find peace. Whether that works for you and me is the question we must face during the suffering we bring with us today or the suffering that will be ours to shoulder on some future occasion.

To be sure, there is peace and solitude to be found out of the chaos of our lives and in the disorienting whirlwind that is God; whether it is our peace will be determined by the dialogue we have with the Creator God. These are matters that call us above the fray of our busy, virtual lives; these are signposts on the way to abundant life that we dare not deprive our children from learning and pursuing of their own free will. We gather here Sunday mornings to honor the world's grievances and the struggle of Job that each of us inevitably faces. Amen.

i. Harold Bloom, *The Daemon Knows*, (Oxford: Oxford University Press, 2015), 135.

– Worship –

Sing, Dance, Love
Psalm 150

June 30, 2013

How fitting Richard that when we sat down Thursday to review the worship service for today we were just receiving news of the Supreme Court's decisions to overturn the Defense of Marriage Act and Proposition 8 in California, thus opening the way for equal rights for and protection of gay and lesbian people under the law of the land.

I mention this because not only does the Court's historic decision resonate with the long-standing vision and work of this congregation to be welcoming and inclusive; and not only because you have personally experienced, if not suffered, as many here today have, the inequalities of the law; but because one component of your vision for what we do when we gather in this sanctuary is to be strengthened and equipped for the work of peace and justice.

But let's start at the beginning, Springfield, Illinois, where your life began with your parents and brother, Tom. There are stories about your prodigious improvisational skill, like weaving the theme of "Happy Birthday to You" into the morning anthem at a church job you had before you could drive a car. You studied organ and conducting at Southern Methodist University, and your first job was chapel organist at West Point. But it was as Music Director of First Presbyterian Church, Tyler, Texas–a large, robust congregation where you served for thirty years–that your vision for worship and music blossomed and you made a name for yourself.

Angels smiled on this congregation when you accepted our offer in 2002 to become Music Director. Your opening act here was to fracture your right arm in a skiing accident–a dangerous sport for musicians except those who play kazoo; but you were from Texas; you hadn't seen snow in three decades, what a great way to get to know and depend upon the compassion and care of this congregation and your amazing, loyal, steadfast assistant Ellie Seib. That was, I am happy to say, the last time you skied.

136

Since then you have taken this choir from strength to strength. Your predecessors, Thomas Swan and Hans Vigeland, both of blessed memory, would take off their hats to you today in honor of what you have accomplished. You have not only preserved the legacy they built making Westminster the premier church choral program of upstate, if not all of New York, but you and this choir have soared to new heights of excellence and achievement. You haven't done it alone, of course. In fact the choir has grown under your leadership, gifted singers want to sing with you, instrumentalists rave about your masterful programming and conducting. But it's you and your passion for making music that attracts them—and the rest of us I might add.

So far, probably against your objection this sermon has been about you; after all it is your day; but my aim is to talk about the essence of worship which is to sing, dance and love. Not theoretically, but as we do it here and as we go out from here on Sunday mornings into our joyful, complicated, challenging, and wonderful lives.

The problem is I can't separate you the person from this our worship; this is true for all of us; worship is not some ethereal, disembodied activity but the concrete expression of humans honoring the gift and source of life. You could expand that statement; you could say, and Calvin did, that anything that we do that we were designed or intended to do is an act of worship. Why? Because it reveals the beauty, power and glory of the Creator. The flip side of this theology is that delicate saying that "God didn't make no junk."

We heard this theology just a few weeks ago from that exquisite duet from Haydn's *Creation* in which the male and female voices of Adam and Eve extol with awe and wonder the mere existence of night and day, earth, wind, air, water, and—praise be to God—*living things*, all of which in their existence illustrate, reveal and point to the power and benevolence of the hand that fashioned them.

One gets the sense watching the maternal behavior of Right Whales and their offspring or King Penguins and their communal impulse or looking into the eyes of your Labrador Retriever or having your hand grasped by a child's as mine was last week following worship, one gets the sense that none of this was inevitable or necessary, nor did it need to happen. Even Darwin himself balked at cold determinism and once observing the bank of a stream, alive with insects and birds and plant life, said, "There is a grandeur to this view of life."

137

What I am saying is that worship isn't something that we are obligated to do or something we invented; it is not for the purpose of entertaining people or giving a stage to performers; rather worship, in its most fundamental form, is what happens when we are true to who we were intended, conceived, and created to be. The word worship means to give honor, dignity, reverence; it means to point to that which is bigger than and beyond oneself.

An artist or engineer or teacher or parent or citizen is worshipping the power and source and beauty of life by living out any of the plethora of roles which we have been equipped, gifted, and inspired to fulfill. Worship in its most basic form is being, living out, embodying who we are called to be and, therefore, it cannot be separated as some detached state of religiosity but has its character and beauty *in and because of* those who are worshipping.

Worship in a sanctuary elegant and grand or spare and simple is a more intentional, more focused act of giving reverence and pointing to the power and source of life. Why would we do that? Because with the capacity to think and be self-aware there is no way not to feel gratitude and awe for what I am calling today the source or ground or power of life. And so we gather in beautiful spaces to offer the best that we have; typically from the arts because the arts such as music and dance and sculpture and painting and poetry are our highest, purest, most noble forms of expression; and before we petition this life force for answers to the vexing messes we've got ourselves into or forgiveness for our blindness to our own and others' wellbeing; before any of that it is first most fitting to sing devotion, admiration, and love for Life with a capital L.

That's why worship takes precedence over everything else that we do and is the reason, the most important reason, we have occupied this space for 159 years, because the moment we lose touch with the power of Life we are lost. And there is much that distracts, and we are easily distracted.

There is another aspect to what happens when people worship that I find mind-boggling. Our faults, our foibles, our weaknesses are often transformed into virtues. Someone who is, let us say, controlling, a stickler for details, perfectionistic will not settle for anything less than the best; behold, standards are kept high; people are challenged to be and do more than they thought possible; the result surprises and enlightens and uplifts. Or say, someone is quick to judge—judgers, the Myers Briggs profile calls them; and they cut through all the withering arguments and uncertainty and reluctant timidity and convince themselves and others to go for it. And the result is bold and serves as a benchmark and confidence-builder for more ministry.

I am not saying this happens all of the time, but I am saying that I have witnessed it happen enough in my life and yours, Richard, and in the lives of others when we are faithful to our calling that I am convinced God uses even the shadow side of our personalities to bring about good in the world. Of course, none of this happens outside of a caring community. I know some people claim to be able to worship God on the golf course, or in a Sunday morning triathlon; I do not quibble with this argument; but without some regularity to participate in that focused, intentional communal form of honoring the source of life we run the risk of the golf course becoming a self-serving idol.

Richard, you are as attuned to the importance of community as any worship leader I have known. We need and depend upon all our gifts from the weekend tenor to the youth reader to the child acolyte, to the voices and prayers of people in the pews including those who cannot even stand to sing because of age or arthritis. Though you are relentless in rehearsal, your compassion for your singers is deep; your relationships with and support of members of the congregation bring hope and healing, fuel our desire to be here, enable us to sing, dance and love yet another day. It's why the Texans come for our annual masterwork and people like the van Bevers from Oregon are here today.

There is an image in the Praise Window along the stairway to your office, Richard. It pictures Albert Schweitzer, the great true-to-his-calling physician, biblical scholar, musician and missionary, sitting, playing at the console of an organ; I say playing not only in the sense of making music but enjoying himself, lost in the beauty of the art. In the lower left-hand corner is a depiction of Schroeder from the cartoon strip *Peanuts* at the keyboard of his miniature concert grand piano in his red and white striped shirt. Little Schroeder in the corner is facing big Al Schweitzer above him; it's as if they are playing to and for and with each other; both lost in the love of music, both lost in the beauty of life, both lost in giving themselves away to that source and gift and power of life that gives them purpose and meaning.

I know now why that's your favorite of all the stained glass in this magnificent room—because that's what you have been doing for us lo these many years from Springfield to West Point to Tyler to here; and we your congregations and colleagues have been doing for you. St. Paul called it love and said it is the greatest of human capacities. It connects, grounds, heals and fulfills. To worship in the basic sense of being faithful to our calling and in the specific sense of what we do when we gather in this room is to love and to love is to worship, point to, and reveal the glory of God.

139

Thank you, dear friend, for helping us to sing, dance and love over these years we have shared. May God bless you in all the years to come. And may you continue to sing, dance and love whereever God leads you. Amen.

– Gun Violence –

Orlando, The American Experiment, And the Politics of Fear
Luke 8:26-39

June 19, 2016

I hope we are still reeling. I hope we haven't gone back to our ordinary day-to-day routine, just yet. The shooting in Orlando only one week ago was a seismic event in the life of our nation; just like all the mass killings before it: an office in San Bernardino, CA; an elementary school in Newtown, CT; a church in Charleston, SC.

We've had fifteen such major mass killings in the past seven years–too many to list in the space of a sermon. The danger is our becoming numb to the carnage. And so, we will read the names of the victims during our prayers today. To hear the names is to let the reality of the loss of life sink-in, below the headlines. It is to put faces on the numbers and to set aside, just for a moment, the furious policy debates and shameful campaign posturing that surround such violence. First and foremost, out of basic human decency and respect, we pay tribute to those who were lost and to their loved ones who grieve.

This past Thursday the President met with each victim's family; those present said he choked up as he listened to them talk about the joy their loved ones brought into their lives; he hugged every person present; there was no sign he wanted to be anywhere else. He is by now the 'consoler in chief' after mass killings; he comforts the grief stricken on our behalf as President but also as a husband and father. We remember today these young adults cut down as they sang and danced, for not to do so would be to allow the violence to define us.

The President's sobering comment that this is a moment to decide what kind of nation we want to be, and that to actively do nothing is to decide, is not just rhetoric. We live in a democracy. We are approaching a critical national election this November; the President's statement went beyond a dysfunctional Congress and its unwillingness to even hold debate on his judicial appointments, his appointments to the Departments of State and

Treasury who actively fight terrorism; and, of course, proposed gun legislation of any kind. The President's call is directed to all of us who have the privilege and responsibility of voting. Sometimes we forget our form of government is an organic, 'living thing.' It began as an improbable experiment. No one knew if 'the people' could govern themselves. Our track record over 240 years is not perfect. But we have been consistently open, inclusive, and committed to preserving the rights allowed for in the Constitution. Those rights are now challenged by the call to close our borders to the members of an entire religion and by attacks on LGBTQ people. The question of governing ourselves is still an open question.

Shift with me to the lesson from Luke today. It is the longest narrative of a healing story in the New Testament. Jesus' ministry has taken him to the outer reaches of Galilee–he is in Gentile territory among swine keepers and a region where demons are numerous and destructive.

The town and the man Jesus encounters have a "settled" arrangement. The man demonstrates what today would be identified as a form of mental illness; consequently, he has been separated from family and friends. The leaders of the town have removed him to a place called 'the tombs.' Out of sight, out of mind. They chain him. Occasionally, he breaks free of the chains, then wanders naked and aimless. This is a community that has learned to live with demonic forces by isolating and partially controlling them. Fred Craddock, the great teacher of the Bible, writes, "the successful balance of tolerance and management of the demonic among this village also allowed the people to keep any attention off their own lives." [i] You know how this goes. Whether in a family, classroom, or group of any size or kind–the ones who have been identified and treated as the 'bad actors' take the attention away from everyone else including those engaging in below the radar violations of acceptable norms and behavior. We worry about the bad person and ignore our own aberrant conduct.

When Jesus calls the demons out of the deranged Gentile, the man becomes rational and sane; the villagers react in fear and anger. You'd think they'd thank Jesus for healing this poor soul–one of their own. But they shun Jesus and tell him to leave their community. You see, Jesus has disrupted their settled arrangement with the dark forces; he has transformed a person who was rejected, marginalized, and labeled. The labels that permitted their exclusion of the man from their society have been overcome. The old definition of who the man was, that literally and socially imprisoned him, is made null and void by the power of Jesus.

142

The old system of defining and dealing with the demons is now impotent and defunct. The deal the village has with the devil has been exposed as unworthy of God's purpose for human life. We don't know if anyone extended friendship to the man who was healed; and though he begs to remain with Jesus, Jesus tells him to return to his home and go into the countryside and proclaim the power of God. But the villagers ask Jesus to leave; there is no telling what broken, oppressive system, family or marriage he might turn to next to expose and expel the forces of darkness. Rather than face themselves and their brokenness, they want him gone.

How does the story relate to us today? To Orlando? It is interesting to consider that while the labels and many of the exclusionary laws and practices about LGBTQ people have been overturned in many states, much of the prejudice and bigotry against LGBTQ people remains intact. The shooting in Orlando is a sobering reminder that LGBTQ people, their allies and friends are not as safe in our society as we may have presumed. The old, settled arrangements around marriage and family life, around sexuality and sexual orientation and gender identity no longer apply. A new, inclusive, pluralistic understanding of human sexuality is making its claim in our society and courts, and in our customs and mores.

The sermon title refers to the politics of fear. Once a person or a community is made vulnerable to their worst fears—fears not squarely faced but inflated and made more ominous and omnipotent than they are—then if you are a politician or leader of any kind you can dictate to the people a path of safety and escape. If they are frightened enough and the politician malevolent, narcissistic and calculating enough, the people will choose routes of escape that violate their own values and principles. They will be blind to the self-serving motives and agenda of the politician; they will not perceive double standards, bigotry or 'conflicts of interest' or others who cynically buy elected officials; they will chant tired slogans bloated with nostalgia and fear; and trust ideologies impervious to common sense, open debate, logic, or the common good.

If this campaign season has revealed anything it has exposed a surprising level of fear in the United States. But it has also tapped into a startling depth of pain and anxiety caused by a stagnant economy. We have heard how our economy has permitted the wealthiest citizens to escalate, beyond imagination, their wealth (and power) while many of those who used to be able to sustain a reasonable quality of life and standard of living have in recent years been unable to do so. Here's an interesting statistic—the average income among the top twenty-five hedge fund managers last year was $500 million and the top two made more than $1.7 billion each. When such numbers are reported, and when we are told that the siphoning off our nation's productivity and wealth among about 1% of the population will have dire long-term economic consequences: more suffering and pain will emerge, causing more people to buy into the politics of fear. The other compelling reason the people of the Gerasene village wanted Jesus gone was because healing the man cost the village a lot of pigs. His exorcism caused an entire herd of swine to rush into the sea. The gospel does stir the economy. Healings, conversions and the embrace of Christian ethics radically influence our getting and spending. The Gerasene people are not praising God that a man was healed, they are counting the cost and finding it too much.

We are at a watershed in American history. On the one hand, our social attitudes and values have reached a critical mass and turning point that have allowed for progressive legislation that even five years ago would have been unimaginable. On the other hand, there is a growing segment of the population that feels left out because they cannot afford daily living expenses, while a few enjoy historic levels of affluence, influence and wealth. These social and economic forces are played out not surprisingly in presidential elections. The first black President and the first female presidential candidate symbolize the power of a diverse and progressive nation. Yet another candidate bullies, demonizes women and people of color, and rejects human rights enshrined in our Constitution to wild and wide acclaim.

If ever there was a good time to live in a democracy it is now. We will—either by actively doing nothing or by our careful and prayerful exercise of our rights and freedoms—shape the direction and destiny of our nation at this ominous fork in the road of our history.

But to simply rally the votes to turn the country in a humane and life-affirming direction will not be enough. We need to exorcise some demons— or invoke the power of God to do so. The bigotry, bias and violence that is fueled by economic fear and suffering will not go away by itself.

What can a church do? Listen and learn. Educate and engage—right here in Buffalo, New York. We don't have to worry about Chicago or New York City; we have enough to keep us busy right here, in our own Gerasene village. We have settled arrangements here in the Queen City that give the illusion we are doing the best we can and poverty and suffering are at least partially under control; But there are people condemned to live in the tombs of our poorest, blighted communities; people we've segregated and manacled with the shackles of economic disparity because of their skin color; others whose sexual orientation is like an iron fetter that prevents them from access to jobs, housing and common fellowship. I know this most recently because of a black pastor from the East Side who described the challenges of a dysfunctional school system, inadequate public transportation, unemployment and debilitating health problems with limited resources as "his world" of ministry.

Listen and learn. Educate and engage. Then let the Spirit move. If we can do that we just might invoke the power of God to call out the demons of prejudice that allow us–right here in this congregation and pulpit–to point to the poor, oppressed, uneducated, condemned members of our community where violence, drug abuse and unemployment fester–and say ain't it awful, then go about our busy lives Monday morning. With some of the subtler and under the radar demons of racism and prejudice gone that white liberal congregations and pastors tend to hold on to, we might find the healing power of God's love at work in *our very midst*. We just might find the American experiment, in this very community, fulfilling those words at the base of the Statue of Liberty–give me your tired, hungry and poor, not to segregate with the crumbs of economic recovery but to welcome into the midst of our opportunity and affluence.

The President is right–we must decide what kind of nation we want to be. Amen.

i. Fred Craddock, *Luke: Bible Commentary for Teaching and Preaching*, (Louisville: John Knox Press, 1990), 117.

– Evangelism –

When God Rolls Up Her Sleeves: Ministry That Matters
John 1:29-42

January 19, 2014

After he graduated from Crozer Theological Seminary in Philadelphia and received a call to ministry and ordination, Martin Luther King, Jr.'s plans to serve the church changed. You see, he was the son of a prominent preacher in Atlanta and he envisioned a life not unlike his father's, leading a prominent, affluent, urban congregation.

But over the course of the next few years another call to ministry took shape. He would encounter the thought of Howard Thurman and Mahatma Gandhi, pursue doctoral studies at Boston University in non-violent social action, then–here was the challenging part–allow himself to get swept up in the emerging movement for racial justice and equality. In a few years he became the movement itself, then risked expanding the movement from racial justice and equality to human justice and equality.

We're talking this month about what happens when God rolls up Her sleeves. I'm not being flippant. The pronoun for the third person of the Trinity, the Spirit, is Sophia, a female pronoun. We're talking what happens when the feminine spirit of God is ignited.

I think of my mother's competent, caring disposition that confronted my father's alcoholism and created a new path for our family. I think of my grade school teachers in Pittsburgh who ran a tight ship and gave me an excellent start in life. I think of the mothers of my friends who created a world of nurture, responsibility and respect in our neighborhood. I think of my sisters who aced their way through school and raised the bar for my early education. I think of my female friends at Yale Divinity School in the first days of women's liberation who cared enough for me that they confronted my blindness to sexism and changed my view of gender roles and relations. I have seen my wife for over thirty years raise our children, work full time, administer our household, care for her aging parents and perform music and yoga–her passions–with utter excellence and grace.

Is it any wonder that the biblical writers refer to the Spirit of God as female! We limit our experience of God if we think of God as only male.

On this weekend honoring Dr. King and in this start to the new year when we are looking at the emergence of the Jesus movement after his birth, I want to consider what it is that ignites *our path* to service and ministry; what happens to us once we are called and then decide to follow Jesus—like Andrew and Simon and the others in this morning's story.

It all begins with John's witness. A noteworthy innovation of this Gospel is that the role of the dove at Jesus' baptism and then the voice of God saying, "This is my son, the beloved," is replaced when John the Baptist takes God's lines and says, "This is he on whom the Spirit has descended, the Son of God." Much depends on John's reliable witness to this revelation of God. The next day Jesus is revealed to him as the Lamb of God. Lamb is a loaded term in the Bible. It stops cold the claims of Christian literalism as Fred Buechner likes to say. Jesus is surely not a lamb! Does John mean the paschal lamb, the lamb sacrificed in the Temple, the Suffering Servant, the lamb of Jewish apocalyptic literature, or some combination of these?

It was John's testimony, and not anything Jesus had said or done so far in his brief appearance in the story, that motivated Andrew and Simon—followers of John—to switch their allegiance to Jesus. The next day Jesus saw Philip and invited him to join them, then Philip reached out to Nathaniel and he joined the emerging cadre of disciples.

It is interesting that three out of the first four of Jesus' followers were *not attracted by Jesus* but by others. Nor did those "others" do anything spectacular but simply identify and point to Jesus. The Spirit took care of the rest. I can't think of a more compelling biblical mandate for us and what we choose or not to say to others about Westminster, about the life we share, about our mission in the community. It raises the question are we witnessing and, if so, how reliable is our witness. I recall a church member who said: "I joined this church because someone remembered my name," then the punch line: *"We are here for people who aren't here yet."* We are here, we might add today, to be reliable witnesses.

And that's where the story begins, after we enter the fold, come into the sphere of Jesus' influence. All of them change: Andrew, Simon, Philip, Nathaniel; Paul knocked off his horse *disappears for three years* while he evolves into a new person. We often forget this detail of his life. Getting knocked off his horse is so much more memorable than disappearing. It is this process of what happens to us once we get knocked off our horse that concerns me today; once we commit to the mission and ministry of a congregation; once we publicly proclaim ourselves to believe in and give priority to the practices of our faith imitating Jesus. The mission of our Spiritual Life Committee and its Sunday programs is exploring this spiritual terrain. So, what happens once we're here?

For starters, a colleague claims that all of us, clergy included, come to church for the wrong reasons. Someone says, "I come to church to find answers for life's deepest questions." Trouble is, in church we read the bible and listening to scripture often leaves us with deeper questions or gives answers we don't like. Someone else says, "I have a demanding job and I come to church for some peace and quiet!" Trouble is, while being with Christ does give us a new sense of peace and well-being, sometimes Jesus agitates us, confuses us, and we come away from church more perplexed than when we arrived. All of which confirms perhaps another truth: Jesus has a way of taking our reasons for being here, for getting involved, and reforming them into better reasons. We come to Jesus, "Just as I am," as the old hymn says, and Jesus receives us, but Jesus rarely leaves us just as we are.

This is precisely what happened to those first followers, to St. Paul, to Dr. King, and, my hunch is, to more than a few of us in this room. Here's what happens: *someone invited us*; we didn't say I am going to explore the metaphysical implications of Christian theology. Rather, someone said why not join me this morning for a special musical worship experience or come help us at the West Side Bazaar or we have a great speaker today in the Case Library. Or we came for answers to some train wreck in our life, longing for that peace and quiet. *And once we get here Jesus, in the presentation or worship or outreach to the community, asks us, just as he did Andrew and Simon, "What are you looking for?"* Which is to say the feminine Spirit of God prompts us deeper.

Thus begins for us as it did for Paul the process of conversion, for lack of a better word. Turning around, re-ordering our priorities; spending less time here and more time there; hanging out with that circle of people rather than this circle of people. Trying things we never tried, getting out of our comfort zone. At one point in his recovery Bill Wilson, founder of AA, had five sponsors whom he turned to, to work on five aspects of his personality he needed to change. Imagine: back-sliding, braggadocio, sell-you-the-Brooklyn Bridge Bill Wilson. His story is the Christian paradox of losing your life to find it in a nutshell: to help himself stay sober in Akron, OH, he walked into the hospital room of fellow drunk Dr. Bob, the other founder, to *help him* stay sober. *Our enlightenment is interdependent with that of others.*

You see, what we originally thought we wanted or needed fades next to the realization that there is more, much more, something much truer both to who we are and to who we are called to become. I have yet to meet the "perfect package"; that is, someone so together or focused that they do not have to grow anymore. In fact, it's often the other way around—the more you grow the more you are aware you need to grow and the more you want to become that whole and authentic person who is your best self.

Our just being here today implies a degree of openness and willingness to engage in that process, and I commend us for it. But that's not all. You see, there is a deep and direct connection between becoming that whole and authentic person and finding our role nudging, pushing the world to become the whole and authentic world God envisions. The two are inextricably linked and interdependent, as Bill Wilson illustrates. Someone once said, our calling is where our great gladness meets the world's deep hunger. I cannot recall any biblical example, historical figure, friend or acquaintance for whom following Jesus led to a narrowing-down of relationships; but rather to a widening-out of them, to a sharper focus on life, a stronger commitment to serve. Self-absorbed piety is not where an encounter with Jesus leads. *Rather we find out where our lives will matter most, then pursue those avenues to places we never thought we'd go.*

A high school friend with his freshly minted Ivy League degree goes to live on the Koinonia Farm in Americus, GA, where Habitat for Humanity got its start. He then goes to work for the startup non-profit. His parents in Pittsburgh are upset with his choice—years later he becomes the director of what had grown into a global service organization. Another friend with a scholarship for wrestling at a Big East university and passion for mathematics, eager to get his MBA and focus his wrestler's discipline on making money, finds himself instead leading a high school youth ministry.

I don't mean to make this sound easy. It's isn't. In fact, it can be a painful, confusing journey. One writer says, "I came to see God's Absence as some strange sense of divine Presence. While God can choose to be absent, there is a form of God's Presence we experience as Absence."

God's Absence can be experienced as a deep longing or wound; as the unfulfilled search for a relationship or experience or dream. Such experiences *are not proof* of God's Absence, but they can be occasions when God seems absent from us. *Then, the only move is to look in some new direction or let go of our longing and see what happens.*

Another way to see the experience of God's Absence is as a "divine protest" against tragedy and evil in the world; a protest against the forces of darkness or fear or isolation that have infiltrated and begun to shape our own lives. And when we let go of the old longing or wound or dream, new space opens, a fertile field for God's emerging Presence in our lives. Congregations go through the same experience when they change some ingrained cultural expectation or behavior.

This movement from God's Absence to God's Presence turned the disciples from would-be cabinet appointees in Jesus' new administration to spreaders of good news, risking their lives to the ends of the earth; Paul gave up being a persecutor of Christians for becoming himself a persecuted Christian; Martin Luther King, Jr., went from a comfortable preacher to a revolutionary prophet first for blacks then for all people.

I'll never forget the story of a pediatric oncologist who described herself as a "pragmatic, post-Christian agnostic." She'd been treating a little girl for most of the little girl's seven years of life. At last the cancer entered its final stage. On the last day, the doctor was in the child's hospital room with the parents and a chaplain who favored psychology over theology. Before she died, the doctor said, the little girl mustered enough energy to sit up and say, 'The angels are so beautiful! Mommy can you see them? Do you hear their singing? Their singing is so beautiful!" Then she lay back on her pillow and died. The girl's parents acted as if they'd been given the most precious gift in the world. The hospital chaplain quickly left the room leaving the agnostic doctor with the grieving Christian family. "Together we contemplated a spiritual mystery that transcended our understanding and experience," the doctor said. For weeks after that day she kept asking herself, "Have *I* found a reliable witness?"

Which brings us back full circle to John's reliable witness to his own disciples. Our wisdom is hopelessly ensnared in the power of darkness. There can be no revelation and, therefore, no witness without freedom from the darkness. Otherwise, all our gods are merely reflections of our own slavery.

Revelation free of the darkness never remains the private possession of John or the disciples or St. Paul or Dr. King or that little girl witnessing to her parents. Like those parents, like all those who've heard the reliable witness of Jesus' followers through the centuries it is nothing less than the precious gift of life and hope we are given. A gift that leads back to its source and out again into the human family; an endless cycle of revelation, witness, conversion, and call to serve in ministry; that's what matters and frees the human family from bondage to its own self-destruction. Amen.

– Vocation –

God Had Other Plans
Acts 9:1-20

April 10, 2016

I recently heard one of my colleagues on the Board of Auburn Seminary share his 'Road to Damascus' story at a dinner he was hosting in his home for board members. Bill is a fifty something retired senior executive from a major bank who moved back to New York a few years ago to start a new chapter in his life. At that time, he and his family were living on the Upper East Side and he was in the habit of driving home each day right past Brick Presbyterian Church at Park Avenue and 90th Street. Bill says that he often noticed the handsome Greek Revival redbrick building but didn't think much about it. You see, Bill was not a "religious" person; he hadn't been raised in the church, and wasn't, he says, looking for a church.

Then one day, as was his habit, he turned the corner at Park and 90th and was passing by the familiar landmark when he 'heard a voice.' By the way, in telling his story, Bill reaffirms that he was of sound body and mind and not in the habit of hearing voices. In fact, he had never before 'heard a voice'–at least, as he did on this day. When he tells the story, still surprised by it, he makes clear the voice he heard was not his own, as if he was 'thinking-to-himself,' but a voice from outside his thoughts or consciousness or memory.

The voice said, "Bill, you can go in there (meaning Brick Presbyterian), they are friendly people." He was not frightened but startled and curious, he says, and the message was so clear–a kind of summons–that he and his wife had no choice but to attend worship at Brick Presbyterian the following Sunday. Long story short, today Bill is an elder at Brick, a board member at Auburn, and the chairperson of Auburn's Profits for Peace. Bill's role with the bank as head of global real estate acquisition and investment perfectly dovetails his role with Profits for Peace. He assembles teams of Christian, Jewish and Muslim venture capitalists to find opportunities for multi-faith investment in regions troubled by religious tension and violence, like the Palestinian territories. His experience and skills at the bank were a perfect fit for the Auburn investors group.

It didn't take long for Bill's pastor at Brick, serving as a kind of Ananias, as we heard in the story from Acts today, to open Bill's eyes to his new life in the Christian community. Michael Lindvahl, Sr. Pastor at Brick, not only oriented Bill and his wife to a Christian congregation and Christian life and values, he steered Bill to Auburn where the banker with no religion today leads one of the most effective non-state sponsored efforts for peace in troubled parts of the world.

When Bill led devotions at one of his first board meetings I could tell that his faith was fresh and passionate. He spoke with discernable gratitude, vigor and awareness of God's presence in his life, and he spoke with humility. His prayer was rare for most of the board or committee meetings I attend in that it was unscripted, came from the heart, and clearly acknowledged that what we were about to do was God's work.

I'll bet if we polled the room today we'd find more than a few 'Road to Damascus' stories; and though we tend to think of Paul's trip on the road to Damascus as rare and remarkable, I'm not so sure that it was. We don't get around in chariots anymore and maybe it isn't always blinding light, but I have talked with some of you and others over the years who have told me about some event, some circumstance that turned you in new and unexpected directions.

Bill and the Apostle Paul belong to different centuries and cultures; Paul was a rigid, judgmental believer who lived to persecute rivals. Bill was an agnostic at best; but they both have this in common—they were re-directed by some presence independent and outside of themselves to use their passion and gifts for the church. Put simply—God gave them work to do. This story is not as much about conversion—you see Paul was already a faithful, practicing Jew— as it is about vocation—finding what it is we are supposed to do, need to do; discovering the place where our deep joy meets the world's deep need, as Fred Buechner says.

But the problem is we do have scales on our eyes and cotton balls in our ears. We live in a society that tells us that everything we want to become or aspire to do derives from our own decision-making and discernment, and that it's all up to us. But the Bible and the experience of God's people is that the other player, the other factor in our life stories, is God. And that's why Paul's story and Bill's story are Easter stories—they are examples of God's presence in our lives as a power greater than us, transcending the allurements of the world, greater than life's dead ends and defeats; a power that directs us to vocation—not necessarily what we do for a living—but the calling to devote our passion and gifts to serve Jesus Christ and his church.

To say that Paul was intense is an understatement. Think Ted Cruz; think Henry VIII's henchman Thomas Cromwell; or Darwin's bulldog Thomas Huxley. Paul was a Pharisee, a purist, someone we'd consider a fundamentalist, for whom life was either black or white; ideological, dogmatic. Paul's business was to persecute Jews who were following the teachings of an uncertified rabbi. Paul thought what he was doing was protecting the faith of Israel from the heretical ideas of outsiders—and yet, he was working against the purposes of God and the universe, not to mention his own best self. At some level perhaps he knew he was misguided; justifying violent acts against innocent people under any circumstances or ideology requires self-deception.

But Paul wasn't going to be stopped with a stern lecture to dial it back. God comes to Paul in a form and language with which he was familiar. God gets Paul's attention with blinding light that knocks Paul off his horse and says: "Saul, Saul why do you persecute me?"/ "Who are you Lord?"/ "I am Jesus, whom you are persecuting. Get up, enter the city and you will be told what you are to do." You see, nuanced language rarely works with dictators and terrorists. God simply out-Paul's Paul. He blinds him, then orders him exactly what to do.

The rest is a fascinating and compelling history: after his rehabilitation Paul preaches good news to religious communities in Damascus; he confounds followers of Jesus who knew and feared him as their persecutor. Paul's passion for purity and practice of faith is redirected. He hangs out at places where he debates followers of other philosophies and faiths. The religious community does not take kindly to what they perceive as his undermining proselytizing. A dead or alive bounty is put on Paul's head—but with the help of his new Christian friends, Paul escapes to Tarsus until things cool down— after which he travels the far reaches of the known world to start churches. Were it not for Paul we would not be here today.

Two points can be made from Bill's and Paul's experiences of being called: first, the voice that speaks is the risen Christ confronting, challenging a person who is headed purely in their own direction which is to say not in the right or best direction; and second, the message is they both ultimately get is: "I have work for you to do."

I've told some of you my own story; it began as a teenager thinking my faith was more about me and evolved into an awareness that following Jesus is really about others. By the time I got to Divinity School I was trying to figure out whether to pursue a career in legal aid, teaching kids who dropped out, or in a distant third place and more out of obligation, parish ministry. It was a big relief when I realized the law and teaching were not where I was being called; those were my own ideas; back then legal aid attorneys were knights in shining armor, and teaching tough kids was a very noble thing to do (still is!); so my path to the ministry involved overcoming my resistance to the church; and while there was no blinding light, there were three voices.

The first voice was a leader in the church I grew up in in Pittsburgh; he said to me out of the blue one day, when I was eight years old, that he had a vision the night before that I was going to be a minister. When I shared the comment with my mother she said, "Oh yes, that nice Mr. Stradley he's very committed to his faith, you can be whatever you want to be honey." The second voice was my high school pastor who said, almost in a whisper, that he strongly urged me to take one year of seminary after college. Both of these voices were completely unexpected and out of context. Nothing I said or did merited their advice. I was a rowdy kid who played hooky from Sunday School and a pretentious jock in high school.

I purposely went to Yale Divinity School because very few of its graduates went into parish ministry; I wanted an open atmosphere to explore my options, to study theology and history; to get hands-on experience in fields outside the church. My first field work assignment was in a legal aid office in New Haven; then in year two I was a teacher's aide in a school for emotionally troubled children. Finally, when I decided to take an intern year in the church, since I had not yet fully explored that possibility, the director of field education assigned me to a pastor he considered the best in the business.

That pastor, Trevor Hauskee, was my Ananias. He helped me see pastoral ministry as a vocation filled with opportunities to do what I wanted to do but couldn't in most other professions—be invited behind the front door of people's homes where people were living. That's where the problems of people I saw in the legal aid office originated—they were coming to get legal band aids, but no real remedies; and home was where kids who didn't fit into traditional classrooms were struggling with parents, siblings and neighbors.

The ministry gives you access to people behind the front door of their homes, Trevor said, as well as credibility in the community—so we started an outreach program to the dozens of people living in halfway houses in that small town; people who'd just been released from a large state psychiatric institution when the first psychotropic drugs made residential programs for many people unnecessary, yet did not equip them to live independently either.

Trevor grew up with missionary parents in China; he marched and was arrested with Dr. King; he and his wife Dorothy were the first feminists I met in any church. Not long into that intern year I was hooked, I knew what I was called to do. A former chaplain of Duke University tells about counseling students consumed with the question, "What should I do with my life?" He tells them to be open to voices other than their own, to sense some claim upon their life other than the claim they personally devise. You could say the same thing to people at any stage of life—because we search throughout our lives for a way to use our passions and gifts—sometimes it's 9 to 5 work we do; sometimes it's a new career, sometimes it's our volunteer service—the key is that it's where God needs us, it's where we belong.

Martin Luther King told the black church in America it existed not for itself but to save the nation from racism. The church's role is not to save itself but to serve the mission and purposes of God. The Constitution of the Presbyterian Church says something quite similar—we are called not to preserve the institution but even to risk losing the institution, to serve God and others; if we live by that principle it frees us up to do daring things, to make a difference.

Here's the good news today: Paul's story is not just Bill's story or Tom Yorty's story, it is your story too. When we open ourselves to embracing God's purpose for our lives we open ourselves to being stopped in our tracks by a voice or a blinding light or a mentor who helps us see needs more vast, possibilities more grand, work more satisfying than we ever imagined in our little scripted plans for ourselves.

Easter is a time to listen and be open to people with unexpected words. They come to remove the scales from our eyes. Resurrection, this year, may be discovering that God has other plans for your life. Amen.

– Democracy –

Sermon on The Mount: Deep Stories
Deuteronomy 30:15-20; 1 Corinthians 3:1-9;
Matthew 5:21-37

February 12, 2017

All three lessons today summon us to the higher ground of restored relationships. _Restored relationships in the nation:_ Moses, in the lesson from Deuteronomy, stands at the Jordan River, just before the people of God surge into the Promised Land. It is an ominous moment because when they take over the land of the Canaanites they will discover not the scarcity of the wilderness but prosperity and abundance that will challenge their ethics and offer alternative sources of power and independence.

Moses is concerned that this new land may talk Israel out of its faith. He alerts the people to this danger by calling upon them to choose the path of life by observing God's commandments, decrees, and ordinances. If they reject the life and faith they learned in the wilderness, he says, they will be on the road to adversity and death. Therefore, in this nation-defining moment, Moses urges, "Choose life!"

Paul calls for _restored relationships in the church._ He observes fighting among groups each claiming to be better than the rest because of the teachers they had. Yet, rather than elevating them, Paul says their division is a sign of spiritual immaturity. No matter who their teacher or how wise, ultimately they serve a God who will use their gifts and efforts to bring about the new world God envisions. Paul appeals to them by comparing their diversity to the parts of a human body and how only through their interdependence and need for one another, like a physical human body, can they be the church God needs them to be. Then in chapter 13, he invites them to give up their childish ways and choose the way of love; to become spiritually whole adults; to experience their best and fullest humanity.

In Matthew, Jesus summons his followers to _restored relationships in daily life_. He interprets the commandments to not murder, steal, lie or commit adultery as not only civil law but moral/ethical standards that are the foundation for a just society. He calls upon his disciples to re-order their relationships not according to the letter of the law that measures external conduct, but according to the intention of the law that speaks to internal motives so that spouses, neighbors, citizens and the poor, all of whom the law accounts for and protects, can flourish in daily relationships aligned with justice. When we aim for the best for each other rather than merely trying to avoid doing the worst to each other relationships are restored.

Moses guides Israel at the beginning of a new epoch in its life as a nation; Paul offers a course correction to the church in Corinth and Jesus' disciples receive a spiritual manifesto that will bring into being the new community, the Kingdom of God. Moses, Paul and Jesus rest their case on how we treat each other and call for right relationships in the church, society and nation. This is the precise biblical definition of 'shalom.' Maybe you're thinking this is all obvious. But we are living in times when it appears we have forgotten the importance of healthy human relationships for the wellbeing of community, from two persons in marriage to the vast enterprise of a nation. The *New Yorker* this past week in an article about the new administration notes that "civilization is immeasurably fragile, and easily turned to brutality and barbarism. The human capacity for hatred is terrifying in its volatility." The identification Friday of Islam and Muslims as the sole source of terrorism, omitting white supremacist and right-wing groups, is a case in point. This past three weeks saw more local demonstrations and protests against the new administration in Washington than any similar period in recent memory. Here at Westminster we held a meeting for a cross section of community leaders to gain a wider perspective on how these abrupt changes of course are affecting us in Western New York.

One person, after a career practicing law, gained what he called reverence for the place of the judiciary in our democracy, and said, like the new Supreme Court nominee, how disheartening it is to hear the president dismiss courts and judges. Another person said he thought after two terms of a black president that we would find ourselves in a 'post-racist, post-antigay, world' but in fact, he said, there is no such post anything world; we are back at the beginning and need to do what we've been attempting to do since the Civil War to end racism and discrimination, but do it better.

One of the Muslims at the table said, "If you all are feeling anxious, imagine how we Muslims feel." An African American who works to improve public education said his community on the East Side is close to the breaking point. A black woman, referring to appointments so out of sync with progressive values as well as the bullying and intimidation that ignites hate crimes across the nation, said, "Now you know what we know and feel what we feel." An executive director of an immigrant resettlement agency talked about families who are unable to look forward to being reunited with loved ones and who are in crisis.

But there was also a sense of gratitude around the table for the chance to listen and learn from one another. The man who works for stronger schools thanked the group and said others' comments will help reshape and refocus his perspective; several noted the value of simply hearing where others are struggling, what their concerns and fears are—as well as their hopes to repair the nation. After the meeting, one of the participants said to me an important voice was missing: the voice of those who support the new administration.

I had to agree and admitted that despite the wide diversity in the room, one thing we all had in common was a negative view of the new White House. Yet, whereas in the past, I would have said that's just fine, we'll never see eye to eye or find common ground, it is increasingly clear to me that unless we can meet with those who hold social/political and economic views opposed to our own we will not repair the breach that severs the nation.

What would it look like to embark on the higher road to restore relationships and heal the great divide in our nation? When we were in Israel recently we met with a Palestinian Christian by the name of Sami Awad. The meeting was in Bethlehem, one of the Palestinian territories you enter through a checkpoint at the security wall. Mr. Awad is the founder of the Holy Land Trust. He told us how his organization is bringing together Jewish settlers and West Bank Muslims. He said their goal is to pursue mutual understanding; to know what it's like to walk in one another's shoes, not through political or theological discussions, but by building real relationships; to get to know one another at a deeper, personal level to build capacity to address the political barriers. "We are not ready to design a two-state map" Sami said "but something important is happening here; people are listening to one another, treating each other with respect." That sure sounds like restoration.

That night we had dinner with residents of Bethlehem in their homes. My small group included our tour guide Yael Friedman—a conservative Jew, mother of three and an Israeli Defense Force combat veteran. She said she had never been in the home of a Palestinian in the territories—in part because our tour with Christians and Jews exploring the geo-politics of Israel was the first such tour she had led. Our Palestinian hosts warmly welcomed us, and before long we were talking about things like parenting, budgeting, doing home repairs, favorite vacation spots, and our hopes and dreams for our children.

By the end of the meal Yael and our host had exchanged email addresses. Yael offered to purchase anything they needed and give it to our host's husband who worked at the Church of the Holy Sepulcher in Jerusalem. Because he is from one of the territories he is not permitted to go anywhere else but his place of work without special permission. So Yael offered to buy household goods, for example, things not available in Bethlehem. She said she would shop for whatever they could not find in Bethlehem and bring it to the Church of the Holy Sepulcher. Two humans who literally live on opposite sides of the wall, reaching out to one another–restored relationship!

But maybe you're saying, well that's Israel. Things are different here. The political chasms here are uniquely unredeemable. But let me tell you about a member of our congregation who shared with me that in her place of work most of the employees voted for Mr. Trump. She said they hold very different views from her own. Then recently she decided to stop eating lunch in her office and take her lunch in the staff break-room to get to know her colleagues better. It's been eye opening. She hears people talk about the ebb and flow of life; she's discovering they share much in common. Like church. This past week she happened to have last Sunday's worship bulletin at the lunch table. When she opened it, her colleagues were impressed a) that she was a regular church-goer and b) that the bulletin includes the full Scripture lessons.

Another foray into what was, before taking lunch with her fellow workers, if not enemy territory, then at least not very welcoming territory. I've been reading Arlie Russell Hochschild's book *Strangers in Their Own Land: Anger and Mourning on the American Right, A Journey to the Heart of Our Political Divide*. Hochschild writes about getting over what she calls the "empathy wall" by seeking to learn and understand our deep stories. Deep stories are about how we experience and feel about the world. Over five years, Hochschild spent time with people in southwest Louisiana in their homes, places of work, VFW halls, barbecues, high school musicals and local diners to find out who they are, what it feels like to live in their shoes. Because she is a professional sociologist she does a lot of supporting research on the region itself, the petro-chemical companies located there, the ecological disasters that have altered life in what they call 'cancer alley', and the state regulations or lack thereof, and what role Baton Rouge has played in the hardscrabble life in Lake Charles, LA. By the end of the book you feel like you understand how these people think and feel, about religion and politics and everything in between.

It's ordination/installation Sunday. Maybe this is a good day to charge our new officers and leaders to help us get to know one another better–starting right here in this congregation; then branching out to our places of work, our neighborhoods. America is not only a nation but also an idea. Pluralism is the centerpiece of that idea. James Madison wrote in the Federalist Papers that having many kinds of faiths and many kinds of people establishes what he called a "multiplicity of interests" to go along with a "multiplicity of religious sects." The core logic of this hallmark principle is that it counters the law of the playground—together many can unite against a bully or a monarch.

There is also an alternative view of America—that it is not an idea but an ethnicity; that of the white Christian men who have dominated it, granting a grudging probationary acceptance to women, or blacks, or immigrants. From Huck Finn's pap as he drank himself to death to General Pickett as he led the charge against Gettysburg to Senator Joe McCarthy it is a view of the world that sees the other as a threat. Restoring everyday relationships, especially with those whose deep stories are different from our own and offer a view of the world that may seem alien to us, is not an exercise in niceness.

Reknitting the bonds of neighbors, linking the suburbs to the urban centers, connecting rural life with city culture may be the most important thing we can do to heal our divided land. Neither side of the aisle in Washington appears to be leading the way. Someone told me the other day he has people who live on his street in one of the south town communities who are "afraid" to come into the city. Democracy is more fragile than we imagined. It's time to peel back the layers and discover the diverse, fascinating stories beneath the labels that divide us. It's what the bible calls us to do. We dare not delay. Amen.

Outrageous Love

Leviticus 19:1-2,9-18; 1 Corinthians 3:10-11; Matthew 5:38-48

February 19, 2017

Did you notice the shift in the reading from Matthew? We are still in the Sermon on the Mount; three Sundays ago, when we started, Jesus was generously distributing God's blessings to the downtrodden and outcast. Generations have found comfort in his promise that those who have been cast down will be blessed and lifted up. But now Jesus turns the tables. He is speaking to the same people, to those same downtrodden and outcast, everyday folks. But he moves from blessings and beatitudes to commands and demands. Jesus shifts from saying what God has done, is doing and will do for you and me to talking about what *we* are expected to do for God. Just what are these commands and demands? Turn your cheek to the one who slaps you, walk the extra mile for the one who imposes upon you. Love your enemy and pray for those who persecute you. In other words resist evil not with evil but with good.

Which sounds a lot like that opening sentence from Leviticus today when Moses says to the people of God—"You must be holy, because I, the Lord your God, am holy." And then Moses defines holiness with a long list of kind and charitable acts that touch every area of life from farming to the court system; in other words, our relationship to God is worked out through our relationships with one another. Moses repeats the great commandments and illustrates them with details like: paying a living wage, leaving some of the harvest for the poor to glean, treating the disabled with courtesy and respect, not abusing legal rights, treating all people the same, standing up for your neighbor, reminding your fellow Israelite of the law so that you are not responsible for their misdeeds, and not holding a grudge. In other words, love your neighbor.

Paul too picks up this theme of living a moral/ethical life and says in today's epistle—we are building on the foundation God has provided. For Moses that foundation was the Law or Torah; for Paul that foundation is the embodiment of the Law in the person of Jesus Christ. Like Jesus in his great sermon and Moses preaching to the people, Paul sends a wakeup call to the members of the Corinthian church. Pay attention to the way you are building on top of God's foundation. No one, no matter how esteemed—from

161

apostles, saints and martyrs of old to the prophets and saints of our time, no one can lay a new foundation. God has already given us the principles we need to live a good life; our purpose is to reveal to the world in our own living what God's principles look like. Here's the key to each of today's readings–add to this strong foundation, this treasure of wisdom, this secret to the abundance of life by being holy as God is holy, by assimilating these values and guidelines for living into your daily conduct and relationships; *not half way but all the way;* not only by treating your neighbor as yourself but by loving even your enemy and praying for those who persecute you.

You may be thinking, "I was with you until that last part about loving my enemy." Outrageous isn't it! What does God expect? Isn't this taking it a bit too far? Science might agree with our skepticism: brain research of the last twenty years has unlocked the secret of our hardwiring. Researchers say that our limbic system is aroused by a set of "hot buttons" that trigger a visceral, intense "danger response."

After millions of years of evolution and social conditioning, our brains tell us to ease in toward potentially rewarding others (like our friends) and to run away from those who are perceived to be dangerous (like our enemies). The adrenaline pumped into our nervous systems to protect us from a perceived enemy makes our responses to external threats kneejerk and defensive. Anxiety forces us into emergency mode, focused only on ourselves and our survival.

Of course, this made sense, from an evolutionary perspective, when our survival could be threatened, suddenly, unexpectedly almost anywhere. When we heard a rustle in the bushes our limbic system enabled us to shift quickly into high gear. This flight/fight response seems fairly descriptive of the dynamics now shaping the political landscape. Both sides treat 'the other'—whether across the political aisle or the person who voted differently across the street or the immigrant from a Muslim nation or a person of color from the other side of town–like a threat or enemy.

Ironically, despite our advanced civilization we live and interact in virtual tribes, dwelling with self-selected, like-minded folks whether in our zip code or online communities. We lump and label 'the other' as enemy often without ever having met or interacted with such a person. Last week at the Auburn board meeting Abbey Disney, granddaughter of Walt, a philanthropist and documentary film maker who produced the prize winning "Pray the Devil Back to Hell" about Muslim and Christian women who joined forces to respond non-violently to the carnage of Civil War in Liberia, Abbey Disney admitted had Trump not been elected she and other likeminded folks would be dancing on the graves of the opposition, not looking back. Hard-wired for survival.

Enter today's Scripture lessons. It is safe to say that our innate coping mechanisms are the source of some of our most damaging mistakes of judgment about others. In a world of hair-trigger nuclear weapons that's not a good thing. Thousands of years of huddling in our tribes equipped us to regard strangers as foes until proven otherwise. In today's interconnected, interdependent world, friend-or-foe fear can certainly be used to manipulate voters but it can also be a great burden and liability.

So if neurological research shows that our visceral, bodily reactions to fear of others are biologically, physiologically rooted, why fight tendencies ingrained in us by millions of years of development? Because the record of God's people proclaims another way: we are not left to our biological impulses and genetic code. God has opened up a new reality; some scientists even credit this alternate reality—call it the morality of love—to evolution itself, but that's another sermon. I wish you could have heard the conversation around the table at Auburn. Questions like how could we have been tone deaf to forty million people; blind to hard-scrabble lives that cobble together two or three part time jobs with no benefits or future?

Someone noted that being out of touch with millions of others—who, for the most part, did not share his liberal/progressive values—reveals aloofness and insensitivity at best and arrogance and presumption at worst. There was talk about 'unlearning' what we've learned in our fast paced, competitive, get ahead culture; relearning things like humility, empathy, making amends versus responding in flight/fight fear.

Around the room, board members were saying they themselves and their friends and colleagues are asking how to hold conversations with those who helped elect the new administration. Many of you have shared similar concerns with me. Heath Rada, a new Auburn board member and immediate past Moderator of the Presbyterian Church USA, said he and his wife have simply not gathered, even socially, with their conservative friends in North Carolina. We are in a rare moment. We realize we have to relearn how to talk with those with whom we disagree. So Auburn is launching a program called "Courageous Conversations" including training 100 people to host dinners in their homes for such brave exchanges.

There are other signs of moving forward to embrace the values of community and inclusivity; to be holy as God is holy, to fight evil with good and not with evil. One month ago, on the anniversary of Martin Luther King, Jr.'s "Letter

163

from a Birmingham Jail," a group of ecumenical leaders issued. "A Letter to White Christians." The letter was written because the white Christian vote (8 in 10 evangelicals, plus a majority of Roman Catholics and Mainline Protestants) was crucial to the election of Mr. Trump, who continues to disparage people of color and anyone who disagrees with him, including the press. The "Letter to White Christians" questions Christian support for a leader who disregards the dignity of so many people. It recognizes that the majority white Christian vote for Mr. Trump sent an unintended message: that white Christians are willing to support someone who perpetuates white supremacy; someone who believes that men have the right to insult and abuse women; who bullies and insults his critics; and who glorifies wealth and success.

The result is that Christianity appears to those not privileged, nor white, nor Christian to be insincere and self-centered rather than the just and generous way of Jesus. But the bible and our faith uphold concern for the least of these, for diversity in the body of Christ, and for unity among God's people, whatever our race, gender or background. The Letter to White Christians calls us to examine our conscience and follow a road that does not build up dividing walls of hostility but destroys them; to turn away from division, fear, and hate and toward those we have neglected with the dignity every human being deserves.

The letter concludes with an appeal to all white Christians whether we voted for Mr. Trump or not: "Do we see how complacent we have been about working for racial justice in our communities? Have we faced the degree to which we benefit from political and social systems that are rigged for people like us and against everyone else? Have we done the inner work to face and turn away from our own deep prejudices based on race, gender, religion and national origin? Have we acknowledged our arrogance and apathy, thinking that since we voted 'the right way' we have no further responsibility to join Jesus in solidarity with those who are poor, marginalized, feared, and hated?"

Here's what fighting evil with good might look like; what being holy as God is holy might translate into: learning the difference between personal racist attitudes and systemic, institutional racism; breaking out of our homogenous bubbles (research says white people have social networks made up of over 90% whites); not putting the burden on non-whites to educate us, but doing our homework with resources readily available to learn what it's like to be a non-white *or a poor white person* in our culture; not tolerating racial labels, stereotypes and slurs. And, finally, preparing ourselves for action, for public witness, to write letters, march in rallies, and put our own skin in the game.

Today's neighbor-oriented lessons, calls us to such action; but I also realize on this President's Day weekend that being able to ask you to consider such action is a gift in this 240-year-old American experiment. There are many nations perhaps, most nations, where such appeals would be considered disloyal to the regime if not illegal. The stakes are high. More than a few articles and essays in the past month have raised concern about global economic crises, nuclear war and climate disaster.

These alarms are not hyperbole. They are legitimate concerns. But today's lessons affirm that we do not need to succumb to fear; rather, we can respond with holiness and love. Radical, outrageous love. Valerie Kaur, a 30 something millennial leader, mother, writer, poet, and proud member of the Sikh faith tradition, founded a national movement called The Revolutionary Love Project. On New Year's Day she preached a sermon in which she referred to the darkness of the tomb as one way to think about the times in which we live. But, she said, she preferred to think of this time as the darkness of the womb–a moment in history when we are called to give birth to something new, a world where our children, where Bryson and his friends here at Westminster, and children across the land can grow up to fullness of strength and stature not in fear of the other but in communities that celebrate difference and practice love of neighbor.

Valerie said midwives tell mothers engaging in the hard work of giving birth to breathe and then to push. That's good advice for us as we face the hard work, in a nation undergoing birthing pangs, of ushering in a just and true society. Breathe, push, breathe, push; let us give birth to a world free of fear where our children can thrive. Breathe. Push. Amen.

– Race Relations –

On the Road to A Better Country
Hebrews 11:8-16

August 7, 2016

The title of the sermon, the thrust of the text today, evoke Jack Kerouac and Willie Nelson and lots of other vagabond, minstrel, innovative, artistic, on the move Americans. The road is a big piece of our national identity. Even though we're two hundred and forty years old we're still young in many ways, willing to go where other nations, nations and cultures far older than the US, are unwilling to tread.

Summer is a time for road trips. Several of you have told me about your travels this summer. We've also made a few as a family—to Long Island for a relative's Muslim ceremony welcoming a new baby; to see old college friends I hadn't seen in over thirty years on the eastern shore of Virginia. Next week my son Douglas and I will caravan to Fort Bragg to move his worldly possessions to Chapel Hill, NC, where he is enrolled to be a student. Then, at the end of August Carol and I and our sainted Labrador retrievers Ninja and Brie will go to New Hampshire to be with our other son, daughter in law, our granddaughter—the amazing Eliza Bea—our granddaughter as well as my sister and brother in law. We've been shouting 'Road Trip!' in our house more than a few times this summer.

You might say that the Bible is one long series of God's people shouting, "Road Trip!"—in nearly every generation, century and millennium since Abraham and Sarah, responding to God's summons, pulled up tent stakes, gathered the livestock and set out on their journey to a promised land. The lesson today from the Book of Hebrews is acutely aware of God's people being sent. In fact, you can make a strong case that faith is defined as the willingness of God's people to go to new places and unknown destinations.

Fred Buechner says, "To journey for the sake of saving our own lives is little by little to cease to live in any sense that really matters, even to ourselves, because it is only journeying for the world's sake—even when it sickens or scares you—that little by little we start to come alive. This was not a conclusion I came to in time," Buechner says, "it was a conclusion from beyond time that came to me." If we get stuck or too sedentary, it could be a sign that

166

we're not living in the Spirit, not keeping a pulse on God's will for our lives; it could be a holy summons to start packing our bags.

We're not reading a Hallmark card or the Travel section of the *Times*. Hebrews says: "By faith Abraham set out...by faith he received power of procreation...from one as good as dead descendants were born...All these died in faith without having received the promises, but from a distance they saw and greeted them. They confessed that they were strangers and foreigners on the earth; for people who speak in this way make it clear that they are seeking a homeland.... they desire a better country."

The implication is that this journey for God, with God, as God's people is what it means to be faithful; it's what we do and who we are. We're talking about the willingness to risk, with eyes wide open, going to an unknown destination. Abraham, writes one scholar, had no idea where he was going when he started out. If we consult the myths and legends of our faith, we find Adam and Eve, Noah and his family and descendants–all of them with itchy feet.

God's people set out not only geographically but also into the interior country–the heartland or land of the heart–where faith takes root, where Israel is born and reborn; where Jesus is constantly knocking on the door; and where he appears to his followers, then sends them to the four corners of the earth. This is faith as journey, as adventure, as willingness. God's people end up in Egypt, become enslaved, then God calls Moses to lead them out into the desert again; they find a homeland, they build a temple, and the super powers invade and scatter them once more. Finally, they come home to their holy land, and Jesus appears to them.

Ecclesiastes says: to everything turn, turn, turn. And the Shaker hymn "Simple Gifts" is about finding 'the valley of love and delight so by turning we come around right.' The story continues here in America. In the 18th century dissident followers of Jesus, people who were not welcome in their own homeland because of their resistance to the Crown, came to a new country where they gave their villages and towns names like New Concord, New Haven, and New York. This nation was settled by people who believed God called them to North America.

In fact, the theme, metaphor and reality of journey is the paramount definition of what it means to be a believer, to be a "follower" of Jesus. The early church referred to our faith as "The Way." We sit here Sundays in a building that looks like it's been here forever. We easily fall into the trap of thinking faith is a static body of information, a codified system of doctrine

167

and that to be faithful is a cognitive process of learning dogma. But the truth is God is constantly calling us, leading us to some new location–getting up to go there is what it means to be faithful.

When I consider my own faith journey, when I look at where I've travelled, there are several trips that have made all the difference. It was the people I met and the experiences I had in the places God called me that made me start to "come alive" in Fred Buechner's terms: from a warm bed to a 6am Bible study in high school; from a huge suburban high school to my small liberal arts Presbyterian college I thought I went to play sports but found my life's calling and vocation; from the rarified academic world of Yale Divinity School to a UCC church on Long Island where we started an outreach ministry to half-way houses for former mental patients; from New Haven to Buffalo the first time which I had to think long and hard about but then met my mentor and dearest friend in ministry who shaped me as a pastor.

It's a long list and includes other journeys from thinking the Bible was a book of answers to life's problems to realizing it's a book about God and God's people; from seeing the church as a place where people get their needs met to see it as a community where people are equipped to serve. You have your stories; I'd love for us to hear them. This past Wednesday we took a road trip to Chautauqua to hear The Reverend Dr. William Barber. There was a good turnout from our friends at the Elmwood Unitarian Universalist Church, Trinity Episcopal Church, and members of St. Paul's Cathedral with Dean Will Mebane, and Canisius College including President John Hurley.

Rev. Barber, you may recall, was one of the keynote speakers at the Democratic National Convention. But before that he was well known throughout the South as the visionary founder of Moral Mondays that began when the legislature of North Carolina instituted new Jim Crow laws making access to the ballot box for blacks and poor white people unconstitutionally difficult. Barber organized and led weekly Monday morning rallies on the steps of the North Carolina State Capital to overturn those laws. And just a week ago, these racist laws were thrown out by a Federal Appeals Court.

Rev. Barber is what Hebrews refers to as a hero of faith; his ministry is one big road trip. The day before Chautauqua he was in Boston; he is now on a fifteen-state preaching tour with Rev. James Forbes and a Gospel choir to encourage blacks and minorities to register for the fall election. He told us his speaking engagement at the DNC was a last-minute invitation; he was there, he thought, to lead a march for poor people and ended up on the podium in the national spotlight. We don't necessarily know the full import or all the reasons why we choose to go to a meeting, a college, or a rally, but chances are good that God wants us there to use us in some way we never expected.

Let me say a bit more about Rev. Barber. His message Wednesday was the subject of his new book–*The Third Reconstruction*. His talk was a scholarly lecture on Constitutional law and American racial history. I would love for us all to read and discuss his book as well as the other recently published, highly acclaimed work of Robert P. Jones *The End of White Christian America*– before November 6. Jones is the visionary founder and leader of the Public Religion Research Institute and is consulted by every media outlet for understanding these complex times. Barber's and Jones' books are uncannily timely and profoundly insightful, hopeful statements for these turbulent times.

The clergy of the Unitarian Church, Trinity Episcopal and I along with Jerry Kelly and John McClive and Voice Buffalo are forming a coalition of white and black churches and community groups to bring William Barber to Buffalo next year. Why? Because we are a poor and heavily segregated city; because Barber is calling for a reframing of the old left/right culture war language; he is putting our challenges in the language of moral imperative; moral imperative is the language of the Bible; it is the language of Jesus' first sermon in Nazareth–preaching good news to the poor, binding up the broken hearted, healing the sick, visiting the prisoner, welcoming the stranger.

The language of the culture wars, Barber says, is too puny for the challenges we face in our cities and nation–we need language big enough to understand and see the path to healing, justice and peace. I mention William Barber because listening to him and meeting him afterwards, it was clear to me that he fits the description of "one who sees and greets the promises of God from a distance." There is a sense that William Barber is a stranger to our time, a person speaking truth to power in a way that few others in our time have spoken.

Barber yearns for a homeland, he has no interest in returning to the land he is departing–he trusts that God has prepared a better place where rich and poor, white and black, gay and straight, male and female—and yes, liberal and conservative—not only co-exist but live together in peace and harmony. When he is asked if this vision of a moral fusion of diverse people, religions and traditions works he tells the story of testing it out in a back-country county in North Carolina populated by military families, Republicans and white folks.

So Barber made a road trip from Raleigh across the state; he thought he was going to test the viability of his moral agenda for North Carolina. He went with trepidation to proclaim his vision for a new homeland. He said he was so scared looking out at that large white audience that he talked and talked, for an hour and forty-five minutes; he was afraid to stop talking for fear of what they would do when he stopped. When he finally did end his remarks, he said their faces were deadpan, expressionless; their clapping barely polite or audible. Then it was Q and A; the first question knocked him over; "Dr. Barber," the questioner asked, "can we start an NAACP chapter here?" Barber is the president of the North Carolina NAACP and he said, "Why, yes, we'd love to have a chapter here in your hometown." Then the questioner asked apologetically, "Can it be all white? You see we just have white folks living here." Barber said he was ready to cry.

Then they asked if he'd be willing to lead them in a march. Still somewhat in disbelief, he asked, "A march to where?" They said they wanted to march to their legislator's home to present a petition for overturning the Jim Crow voting laws. Barber said, "I'd be honored. When do you want to march? "Tonight!" they shouted." Barber with just a vestige of racial fear said, "Black folks don't usually lead marches in white communities in the south at night. Let's march tomorrow afternoon," he said, "and I'll have other chapters here to join us." Finally, someone rose to tell Rev. Barber that they invited him to come talk to them because they wanted to make sure he and his program were substantive and committed. "Does this moral fusion of people and faith traditions bridging all the social divides including liberal and conservative work?" he asked rhetorically at Chautauqua? "Yes, it works!" he said, to a standing ovation of that nearly all white, conservative Chautauqua audience, "Yes, it works!"

The message today is this: faith is a journey; God calls us to places we may not prefer or choose to go; nor do we always know exactly why we are going. But we go with confidence and trust, searching for a homeland, greeting the promises of God from afar, going to unknown destinations with eyes wide open. Amen.

– July Fourth –

Front Row Seat to New Life
Luke 10:1-11, 16-20

July 3, 2016

Two hundred and forty years ago yesterday the Second Continental Congress assembled in Philadelphia to formally adopt a resolution for independence from Great Britain. The vote was unanimous with, interestingly, *New York* abstaining. The colonies had been warring with England for over a year because of steep taxes plus the fact that they were being ruled by a king an ocean away. Some wanted to remain under British rule, but most did not. Thomas Paine's pamphlet *Common Sense,* which sold over 500,000 copies, generated a groundswell of support for independence. Among his observations, Paine also noted that the King was a brute.

A month prior to passage of the resolution to leave Great Britain, when the motion was first presented to Congress on June 5, a committee of five including John Adams, Thomas Jefferson and Ben Franklin was appointed for drafting what became The Declaration of Independence. Adams proposed Jefferson as chief writer because Adams—in his own words— was 'obnoxious, suspect and unpopular', whereas Jefferson was much the opposite. Jefferson wrote the document in just seventeen days on a small, portable writing desk of his own design and manufacture. The final draft was approved, after minor tinkering from the committee, on July 4.[i]

Fast forward to election year of 2016. Democracy is rarely a neat and tidy business. I remember hearing the House of Commons debate some controversial issue and I was appalled at the beer hall nature of the shouting and disagreement. Indeed, we here in the US regularly give the world a remarkable display of rude and crude governing. From our own Congress to some of the candidates for elected office, including those running for President, our public discourse seems well below the level of debate and discussion of our founders. While they used language every bit as colorful as anyone since, it was their grasp of and attention to great ideas that distinguished them. Sam Tanenhaus wrote, in a recent essay and review of eight new books that offer insight into the present political climate, that the low-ebb of populist anger and political posturing we are now witnessing is not unique to our generation but has strong precedent in our national history.

The presidential elections of 1976, 1968 and 1936 also experienced among them split parties, chaos and violence and populist rage manipulated by authoritarian candidates for office. I want to explore with you on this Fourth of July weekend not just the historical context in which the political pendulum of the nation swings but also the cultural landscape in which we work out for better or worse our life together. And central to that cultural reality that shapes us as a nation is the role of religion and religious institutions like Westminster.

Arthur Schlesinger Jr., for example, commenting on the presidential election of 1936, wrote that the populist audience for that election mostly came from "the old lower-middle classes, in an unprecedented stage of frustration and fear [and] menace[d] by humiliation, dispossession and poverty."

"They came," he said, "from provincial and traditionally nonpolitical groups, jolted from apathy into near hysteria by the shock of economic collapse." "And," he continued, "many also came from the evangelical denominations in which years of bible reading and fundamentalist revivalism accustomed them to millennial solutions."[ii]

If you go back to the beginning of the republic and earlier–the popular narratives that drove the push to the new world, shaped the identity of the young nation, and served as a moral compass for the national consciousness were biblically based stories and values. Ideas like identifying the North American wilderness as the new Eden, and the first colonialists as the new Adam, and the new nation as God's chosen people called to be a light to all the nations–a city on a hill–manifesting a destiny ordained by God in this new promised land for the purpose of redeeming a corrupt Old World Europe–all of these images and themes if not world views were fashioned by 18th and 19th century religious and political leaders–especially during the First and Second Great Awakenings.

If the new nation was not technically Christian given the new constitution's allowance for freedom of religious expression and allusions to the deistic nature of God in our Constitution and Bill of Rights, *the popular narrative of our origin and purpose* was clearly an adaptation of Judeo-Christian biblical themes by and for religious dissidents who settled the land and then popular preachers who perpetuated the mantle of God's blessing upon our national experiment.

Until recently, it has been hard to separate our national identity from Christian values and ideals. But today we are the most religiously diverse nation in the world, and for the first time there is a decline in those claiming any religious affiliation. Gallup's annual poll still documents a high degree of identification of the population with belief in God, the practice of prayer and church attendance. Indeed, the number of self-identified practicing Christians has remained impressively high especially compared to such numbers in other developed nations.

But times change. If you were around in the '50s, the post WWII baby boom era, you remember how full virtually every church sanctuary was; and how white, or black, since Christian churches then and now remain mostly racially segregated. Prior to 1960 the Presbyterian Church was known as the Republican Party at Prayer—a designation that today would not be even close to accurate. It was in the '60s that the breakdown of the old Protestant, Catholic, Jew definition of the nation's predominant religious bodies gave way to the defining characteristic of religious communities not by faith tradition but as politically liberal or conservative.

The importance of this restructuring of American religion is hard to overestimate. It enabled the election of our first Catholic President in 1960 and our first born again President in 1976, and fueled the anti-war and civil rights movements. After that, it formed a powerful coalition of religiously and politically conservative groups and voters that elected Ronald Reagan in 1980 and served as voting blocks that ushered George Herbert Bush, Bill Clinton and George Walker Bush into office.

But times change. Just this month, a new study by Robert Jones of the Public Religion Research Institute titled *The End of White Protestant America* marks a major shift in the religious and political fabric of the country. Jones' work, based on extensive survey and interview data, documents that white Protestants are no longer the American majority, and the cultural and institutional world they built no longer sits at the center of American public life. In 1993, for example, the year Bill Clinton took office, 51% of Americans identified as white Protestants. In 2014, that percentage dropped to 32%. Not to mention millennials who stream for the church exit, turned off by the intolerant 'anti-gay teachings' thundered from many evangelical pulpits. Those church-goers left behind, Jones writes, stew in the bitter juices of 'cultural loss' and yearn for yesterday.

Jones' research tracks increasing feelings of nostalgia and unease in a world fraught with terrorist violence and vulnerable economies. He documents longing among growing numbers of white Americans for a simpler time as well as protection from foreign threat and influence and a preference among many for more authoritarian leaders; even leaders who are willing to break the rules in dealing with these issues.

Hand in hand with the shrinkage of white Protestant America is a growing opinion representing the majority among white evangelicals, Republicans and Trump supporters that white Americans are as discriminated against as black and minority Americans. Only 39% of the general population holds the same view.[iii] My hunch is many of us might have guessed or predicted the trends Jones documents, but to see how rapidly and virulently the cultural wars are marching into this new phase of race and class difference, especially in the current presidential campaign, is something of a wakeup call.

Responses range from the atheists who rejoice at any dent in the cultural credibility and authority of the church to many congregations and church leaders in the mode of retreat and survival who condemn a society gone astray from Christian values who now lobby in the wake of gay rights for church-sanctioned bigotry under the euphemism of 'religious liberty.' But have you noticed that Westminster and congregations like us do not fit the reactionary trends of a shrinking white Protestant population? This morning's story of Jesus' sending out of the Seventy to gather the harvest of new believers offers a compelling charge for progressive mainline churches in America like us.

This story appears only in Luke, whose gospel is devoted to the downtrodden and outcast who, unlike bickering disciples or clueless religious authorities, "get the faith." Culturally displaced white, progressive Protestant Americans may be able to relate. Jesus himself says, "the harvest is plentiful, but the laborers are few." We understand that the laborers are few, but where, we might ask, is this harvest if we see a white Protestant church shrinking and disappearing? It is worth remembering that while Luke is speaking to those who are mostly outcast because of their disease or gender or occupation or economic status or ethnic identity they are nevertheless a diverse audience. The ones he appeals to, to go into the field and reap the harvest, represent the diversity of the human family.

I had breakfast last week with a good friend who is a white Pentecostal pastor of two congregations of African immigrants. Bob walks the walk. He is fond of quoting Gustavo Gutierrez, the Peruvian liberation theologian and priest who said that the test of mission and ministry is our friendship with the poor. A landmark book titled *When Helping Hurts* published in 2009, elaborates on Gutierrez's friendship test for mission. Poverty will change, the authors say, depending on who is defining it. While the poor will define poverty more in social terms, wealthy churches, most white Protestants, define poverty as a lack of material things or geographical location. This creates a harmful cycle where mission is seen as a top down doling out of material resources (which reinforces a sense of inferiority and lack of self-esteem among the poor) rather than a true partnership in which both parties give and take. WEDI is a model for the latter. The more members a congregation deploys (which is another word for what Jesus did sending the Seventy), the more that congregation will thrive and reap a great harvest.

We are in a very different place as Presbyterians in 2016 than in 1968 or 1950. Much has stayed the same—this beautiful sanctuary, our Aeolian Skinner organs, our traditional worship—but tectonic shifts have changed the culture and face of America. People no longer stream into our sanctuary because it is the only option on a Sunday morning; nor can we focus only on political causes without paying attention to the spiritual needs that sustain us.

William Barber, the North Carolina preacher we're going to Chautauqua on August 3rd to hear is, many say, a new Martin Luther King, Jr. He is calling for a fusion, a fellowship, a friendship in Gutierrez's terms, of like-minded, diverse people; an 'e pluribus unum' of black and white; Democrat, Republican, Independent; poor, affluent, gay and straight to rebuild the nation around moral values that reject exclusion from the ballot box or payroll or reject opportunity because of skin color or sexual orientation or religious persuasion.

This is the new harvest Jesus is sending us out to reap. White Protestant churches who have ears to hear let them hear. If old Tom Jefferson were with us today, he'd say, 'that's what we had in mind from the start.' Amen.

i. Garrison Keillor, *Writer's Almanac*, July 2, 2016.
ii. Sam Tanenhaus, "Why Populism Now?" *The New York Times Book Review*, Sunday June 26, 2016, p 14-17.
iii. Tanenhaus, 14-17.

– Gay Pride –

Discombobulating the Grim Reaper
Luke 7: 11-17

June 5, 2016

This Sunday is Gay Pride Day across the nation. Earlier this week the President declared June Gay Pride Month. His proclamation states, "Since our founding, America has advanced on an unending path toward becoming a more perfect Union. This journey, led by forward-thinking individuals who have set their sights on reaching for a brighter tomorrow, has never been easy or smooth. The fight for dignity and equality for lesbian, gay, bisexual and transgender people is reflected in the tireless dedication of advocates and allies who strive to forge a more inclusive society. They have spurred sweeping progress by changing hearts and minds and by demanding equal treatment—under our laws, from our courts and in our politics. This month we recognize all they have done to bring us to this point, and we recommit to bending the arc of our Nation toward justice."

It is a privilege to pastor a congregation that has been and continues to be part of that journey and commitment to bend the arc of the Nation toward justice. And while there was much rejoicing when the Supreme Court overturned the Defense of Marriage and Family Act in 2014, thus ensuring the right to same sex marriage, there is more recently a new debate over the rights of transgender people. North Carolina has been the center of the storm, but other states and politicians have lined up against this new iteration of sexual justice—the right of transgender people to use the bathroom of their self-identified gender.

More than a few, mostly in southern states, have chimed in from their perches in governor's mansions and state legislatures in support of North Carolina's stand against a national and global chorus of voices for inclusivity. The episode is eerily reminiscent of the exclusion, a generation ago, of African-Americans from lunch counters, buses, drinking fountains and bathrooms reserved for "whites only." The fact that the first black female Attorney General of the United States is suing the State of North Carolina for discrimination to public access is poetic justice. Her lawsuit recalls the days of Jim Crow when North Carolina was perfectly happy with 'all-gender' bathrooms as the only bathrooms for male and female blacks prohibited from using 'white only' facilities.

Someone has said the adage "everything new is old again" has been reversed by the goings-on in North Carolina; indeed, it would seem there, over the transgender issues, everything old is new again; discrimination, bigotry and bias die hard. In fact, the same tired arguments are being dragged out yet again, as Jelani Cobb of *The New Yorker* writes: "As with the discrimination of the past, the lines between victim and victimizer are [now] deliberately blurred [in NC]. Jim Crow was anchored in a sense of white victimhood and fevered arguments about the protection of white women from black male rapists. Today–the new imagined predator is a transgender male."

Gay Pride Day is an important annual reminder that we are members of a rainbow species–that diversity is a God-given gift to the human family and, therefore, to recognize and celebrate our diversity is to fully recognize and celebrate creation as God made it–for which the psalmist sings, "majestic is his name in all the earth." It is fitting that our celebration extends beyond gay and lesbian matters to include transgender identity. I suspect most of us have more to learn about what transgender is and means. This sermon is an attempt to get that project on our radar. It would be good if one of our education committees chose to deal with human sexuality and the politics of justice in the 21st century. But that said, today is a day to acknowledge the progress that has been made in LGBT justice and that there is also a long way to go in gender rights and freedoms.

Such as justice for women; we have a false sense that women have essentially achieved equal rights at least with job opportunity, that a young girl can be anything she wants to be; yet, while much progress has been made there are grave concerns about the social and cultural oppression and abuse of women–everywhere. Gloria Steinem in an interview last week reported that for the first time in history there are fewer females than males in the world due to the wide-spread, systematic, methodical and routine violence perpetrated against women in all societies, especially developing nations. Studies confirm that there is more violence against females of every age group where families, communities, societies, and nations rigidly define the social roles of men and women. Conversely, in social groupings where there is more integration of social roles, where men and women share and have in common more tasks and functions, there is less oppression and violence.

Consider the Scripture lesson this morning; it is a reminder that the status of women in the ancient world was on the lowest rung on the social ladder–as it still is in many societies. Jesus has compassion because he sees it is a widow who is the mother of the young man who has died. He knows her life has been cut off not just from family—for he was an only child—but also from any economic or material survival.

177

Luke's lesson is more about the mother than the son whom Jesus raises from the dead. It is interesting this story comes about six weeks after Easter–the average length of time it takes for the death of a loved one or friend to sink in. The six-week mark is when the daily routine without the loved one becomes the new reality. When the realization that this is the way it will be displaces whatever fantasies or embers of hope of seeing the loved one again that may exist. Despite the uproar at Easter and the resurrection, deep down we may suspect that nothing has changed. Caesar is still in charge. We're still having funerals. All the old distinctions–male/female, rich/poor, young/old–are still in place. We brush ourselves off after Easter and continue our trek that ends in death. We set goals, work hard, accumulate stuff, and build our walls for security, but in the end death waits; grinning, ultimately victorious.

And not just at the end but the big and little deaths through life. Some of our most painful dead ends come before death. Illness and disease are often dress rehearsals for death, simulations of that time when we will be cut off from the land of the living, isolated and alone. Or there's an unexpected meeting and the boss tells you that you and the company have come to a parting of the roads; or you get the letter that says not, "Congratulations, you're accepted!" but "We regret to inform you…" Or like Roger Angell, the 96 old baseball writer/former editor of the *The New Yorker* whose essay entitled, "This Old Man" is one of the most poignant meditations on aging and death I have ever read, we experience losses of family members, friends and even our beloved pets to the grim drum beat of tolls and statistics of death from wars, terrorism, natural disasters and crime.

Last night on the steps of the Historical Society, facing the Japanese Garden I had the privilege of saying the invocation for the first annual "Save the Michaels of the World" memorial service for family members and friends who have lost loved ones to opioid addiction. This is an epidemic greater than the AIDS epidemic in the 1980s.

Parents, brothers, sisters and friends told the heart-breaking stories of their loved one's addiction and death–young men and women, regardless of status or condition, who were prescribed pain killers and either abused them or turned to heroin and alcohol when they were no longer prescribed.

Avi and Julie Israel's son Michael—a brilliant engineering student at the University of Buffalo—took his life five years ago after living on pain medication for most of his teenage life for Crones disease. He despaired of being able to wean himself from the painkillers. The Israels started "Save the

Michaels of the World" to raise awareness and fix a broken and sinister system of pharmaceutical pain management.

Teach us to number our days, says the Psalmist, "so we can have a wise heart." Numbered days and a wise heart. This is the way we talk and walk on this journey through what Angell calls "the collapsing, grossly insistent world." Yet today we are in the company of Jesus, so it is good to fasten our seat belts and hold onto our hats. Jesus by now is attracting crowds of the curious and the committed. As Jesus and his entourage enter the village, the funeral procession with the grieving, widowed, now childless mother is leaving the village and they encounter one another. Jesus sees what is going on. He has compassion for the woman. He understands that her world is lost and feels her profound despair.

He tells her not to cry; it is an instruction as baffling as his informing Martha and Mary that their brother is not dead. How do you tell a grieving person not to cry? What is Jesus up to? Then to the young man who is dead, he says, "Rise!" Who instructs a dead man to rise? The man sits up and begins to speak; fear seizes everyone. Is your seat belt fastened? Now that Jesus has intruded among us God can surprise us anytime God pleases, pushing into "off limits" territory; the regions death thought it owned.

Sometimes the surprising work of Jesus among us is glorious, sometimes scary, sometimes both. What we thought was a dead end isn't a dead end but a turn in the road that leads to life. One theologian says the way you can tell the difference between a false, dead god, an idol, and a true and living God– like the one who disrupted the funeral procession in Nain–is that an idol, a dead god, is one we concoct ourselves; a dead god is controllable, containable, manageable; a dead god stays put and can be used for our purposes. But a living God shocks, turns things upside down, and uses us for God's purposes.

As the President said in his proclamation of Gay Pride Month, a lot of people are working for LGBT justice, and, we could add, a lot of people are working for all kinds of justice–for equal rights for women; for those facing addiction– to name just a few this morning. And among all of those brave souls, those who call themselves followers of Jesus have a special place.

We do this work because he summons us to repel the forces of darkness. We live in times as challenging to human rights, freedom and wellbeing as any since WWII; from LGBT equality to the need for more women in positions of power and authority to the longing for a health care industry that does not abuse the sick for profit–we are waging battles of life and death. We may be

179

discouraged or fatigued or weary. Last night Avi Israel shared with me that when he visited Congressman Brian Higgins, he was told he was taking on a $2.7 trillion industry and not to get his hopes up. But I am sure that's what they said to other everyday, ordinary people whose loved ones or who themselves were excluded or abused or exploited by some rigged system. There were hundreds of people at the gathering last night who emerged from their tombs of shame and guilt wearing bright t-shirts with their loved ones' smiling faces on them.

The message today is we need not despair in the work for justice because the God we worship is a living God; a God who disrupted our settled arrangements with death in a little village outside of Capernaum. As one elder said to the session after a long debate over limited resources and money, "Friends, since the resurrection it's hard for us to know what can and can't happen in the church."

We can never predict to what or where the fellowship of this table will lead us—except that it will change hearts, heal brokenness, and quell fear. When you walk with Jesus, the old order of death we thought so invincible crumbles; walls fall, barriers disappear. "Rise up," he said to the young man on the funeral bier. Indeed, rise up! Amen.

Witness

Acts 1:6-14

June 1, 2014

This past Friday was the 92nd anniversary of the dedication of the Lincoln Memorial in Washington, DC. Conceived in 1867, construction on the project did not start until 1914. It was designed by Henry Bacon to resemble the Pantheon—the first century temple in Rome dedicated to Roman pagan gods; its thirty-six columns represent the thirty-six states in the union at the time of Lincoln's assassination. On the south wall is inscribed the Gettysburg Address. The sculptor, Daniel Chester French, is rumored to have evoked the profile of Robert E. Lee in the locks of Lincoln's hair.

Yet despite the Memorial's grandeur, one fact about its dedication serves as a harsh reminder that as far as we think we might progress, the work of justice is never finished. The fact is this: even though Lincoln was known as the Great Emancipator, the audience of 50,000 for the dedication on May 30, 1922 was segregated; and the keynote speaker Robert Moton, president of the Tuskegee Institute and an African-American, was not permitted to sit on the speakers' platform.

Even after slavery had been abolished *constitutionally*, the bias, bigotry and violence upon which it was built continued in the Jim Crow laws of the south; not to mention the commonplace lynchings of black men in southern and western states. In fact, an anti-lynching bill was *defeated* in Congress in 1922 after a block of white southern Democrats filibustered the effort.

From the standpoint of history, it is easy to look back and wonder how it was possible for people to live with such social and political dissonance. I mean what did the people in the crowd that day who came to witness the dedication of the Lincoln Memorial say to themselves about the segregated audience? What did they think when the keynote speaker, a black man, had to approach the podium from his place among the blacks, segregated from the white audience? How could they both honor Lincoln and participate in the ceremonies that day?

No doubt future generations will look back on our generation and ask similar questions about our integrity as free men and women living in the world's leading democracy while racism, gender bias, LGBT discrimination, gun violence and climate change continue unchallenged in much of our daily life. That is why days like today–More Light Sunday and the Gay Pride Parade – are so important.

As a congregation, 30 years ago this year, we joined a small and fledgling movement called "More Light." We said we wanted to bring more light on the topic of gay and lesbian discrimination, we said we wanted to be open to and welcoming of gay and lesbian people and invite them to full participation in the life of this church. We were accused of violating the church's constitution and defended ourselves in the courts of the church all the way to the national judicial body.

When you witness the Gay Pride Parade today and see the colorful, flamboyant, even outrageous expression of sexual identity and orientation; the free and uninhibited demonstration of conjugal love of women for women and men for men remember that there are those who are gay, lesbian, bisexual and transgender who live closeted lives; those who live in fear of being discovered; in many cases even their families and loved ones live closeted, fearful lives. Remember that there are many today, in 2014, bound by the fear of rejection, of violence, of embracing their inherent life *because of their sexual orientation* and, therefore, they keep this fundamental aspect of their humanity a secret.

The Gay Pride Parade which takes place in many cities is really a civil rights march–recalling those parades in Selma, Birmingham and Skokie, Illinois, when Dr. King walked arms linked with white and black brothers and sisters for equal rights, for civil rights, for the full right of freedom. Today's parade says, 'do not be afraid, do not live in fear.'

The title of the sermon today is witness. In the story from Acts, Jesus said that his followers would be his witnesses in Jerusalem and to the ends of the earth. The word "witness" can mean either simply passively observing an event or, for our purposes this morning, more importantly, it can mean paying tribute to a truth, a principle, a matter of justice through one's words and actions.

Back in 1922, the 50,000 people who showed up at the Lincoln Memorial witnessed the dedication of a monument. But forty years later, in 1962, when 250,000 people gathered from across the nation to fill the mall–from the columns of Lincoln's Memorial to the Washington Monument–to hear Dr. King preach his "I have a dream" sermon, *they were witnessing* to the truth of a world where racial diversity was embraced and celebrated rather than segregated and shunned.

182

What is it that transforms people from being passive witnesses to what merely goes on in the world around us into brave and active witnesses for truth and justice? I give you today's reading from the Book of Acts. When the disciples gathered in Jerusalem and asked the risen Christ, "Lord, is this the time when you will restore the kingdom to Israel?" he said to them, "It is not for you to know the times or periods that God has set by his authority. But you will receive power when the Holy Spirit comes upon you; and you will be my witnesses in Jerusalem and to the ends of the earth."

The next scene in Acts is of the disciples and the women returning from Mt. Olivet, where Christ departed from them as if into heaven ,to Jerusalem, to the upper room. This is the church forming in embryo. The Holy Spirit had not yet come but something was happening to those disciples; they were beginning to change inwardly, personally; but also outwardly in their decisions and behavior. They were shifting from passive observers of Jesus to his active representatives in the world. And this: a collective identity was emerging. They decided to stick together; the women played as much a role as the men. What did they do? They prayed, says Acts.

One week later the Holy Spirit descended; their mission was clearly defined, they would be on fire with what became their abiding passion for bringing light into a dark world which. Why? Because on the one hand, they knew deeply and personally how fear strangles life; but on the other hand, they knew personally and deeply the liberation from fear the risen Christ offers.

And so they were not just willing *but went relentlessly* to the ends of the earth to free the world from fear. It is not too much to say that we are here today because a handful of men and women dedicated themselves to telling the story of Jesus as far and as wide as they possibly could.

There is really only one thing that animates, enlivens and makes a church– God's Spirit of liberation and life that swept through the hearts of those first followers. It is that same Spirit that swept through the hearts of the leaders and participants of the Reformation, and of the Abolition and the Civil Rights movements. This is the same Spirit that swept through the hearts of the members of *this church* thirty years ago when we decided to become a More Light congregation.

Maya Angelou, now of blessed memory, witnessed to that power of life at work in her own life when she wrote: Out of the huts of history's shame/I rise/Up from the past that's rooted in pain/I rise/I'm a black ocean, leaping and wide/Welling and swelling I bear in the tide/Leaving behind nights of terror and fear/I rise/Into a daybreak that's wondrously clear/I

183

rise/Bringing the gifts that my ancestors gave/I am the dream and the hope of the slave/I rise/I rise/I rise.

Fitting words for Ascension and More Light Sunday. It's good to recall how this congregation *rose to the occasion* and witnessed to the power of life and God's truth and justice thirty years ago when LGBT rights stood in peril. But looking back is only half of our task today. The second half of our task is to see where people still live in darkness and fear and the work of justice remains unfinished; and then to listen for God's call to be witnesses and go as near or far as it takes us. Amen.

– Summer –

View from The Porch: Song of Solomon
Song of Solomon 2:8-13

September 2, 2012

Let's get right to the point: that was some pretty hot poetry we just heard Mary Beth read. "Arise, my love, my fair one, and come away; for now the winter is past, the rain is over and gone. The flowers appear on the earth; the time of singing has come, the voice of the turtledove is heard in our land. The fig tree puts forth its figs, the vines are in blossom, they give forth fragrance. Arise, my love, my fair one, come away."

According to the rabbis, the Song of Solomon was the subject of considerable debate among the sages at Jamnia who, in the year 90 CE, conferred their approval on what we now call the canon or collection of books in the Hebrew bible. Their issue: the pure, sensual, sexual language and imagery of this poetry. It drips physical desire; the raw, earthy attraction of two humans for one another; the longing to become one, to meet in union, in completion. Whoever said the Bible is boring apparently did not read the Song of Solomon.

The best exegetes say this poetry is intended not to be taken literally or figuratively but *both* literally *and* figuratively for it is an unabashed celebration of creation and of the human impulse to perpetuate life, as well as the simple, powerful urge to immerse one's being in the joy and celebration of consummated love.

Today's text is perfect for this annual Labor Day sermon from the porch of our cottage at Lake Winnipesaukee. My hunch is you have some porch or tree or location in nature where the vista of life in summer and life in general stretches out before you. These places are essential to our health and well-being.

It was nothing if not sensual to sit each morning in the chaise lounge, coffee in hand, on the screened-in porch attached to the lakeside of the house perched on a steep bank overlooking Alton Bay. The porch is held high off the ground by pillars making a virtual tree house two stories up, surrounded by pine boughs and deciduous foliage.

There I began the day wrapped in a blanket against the cool air; the lake like glass below, the canopy of trees above lighted by the rising sun; a perfect place to pray. My prayers included us individually and together to become the people, church, mission and school God beckons; comfort for those afflicted in our community and world–which sadly, this summer, constitutes a long list who grieve the recent loss of loved ones and some who face life-threatening illnesses; and my prayers included, certainly, family and friends.

These were the intimate conversations that started my day with our lover, creator God; the One who pursues, cherishes and ravishes us. Conversations like the conversation I overheard staying with old friends in Easton, PA, last week. Coming downstairs early in pursuit of coffee I saw the two of them in the living room cuddled on the couch in their pajamas speaking in the low, soft tones and occasional laughter of lovers who have shared and shaped one another's lives.

My morning time in NH was like that: giving thanks; pouring out what was on my heart; looking to the day ahead. The Bible tells us again and again that our God is personal, loving, and involved, pursuing us unrelentingly until she captures our hearts and elicits our devotion.

The notion that "for Christianity to be relevant and believable to thinking people the notion of a personal, interventionist God must change" does not account for the poetry of the Song of Solomon; nor for the ancient image of the church as the "bride" of Christ; nor for the beloved story of a young woman who submits herself to be a fellow conspirator in God's dramatic, miraculous intervention with the human family through a son she would bear called Emmanuel, "God With Us". If this great God is not personal and does not intervene then how do we explain such language as: he is the shepherd, we are the sheep; he is the vine, we are the branches; he is the bread, we feed on him; he is the living water who quenches our thirst forever; she gathers us under her wings like a mother hen.

Almost never, in the biblical account, does God seek merely our intellectual assent but wants all of us–mind, body and spirit. God's goal for us is the goal of a lover: intimate, mutual dwelling together, *indwelling* so that, like seasoned and loving partners who can complete each other's sentences and anticipate one another's needs, St. Paul could say "not I but the Christ who lives in me."

Sitting on that porch each morning in the quiet at sunrise, being at one with the living, breathing world around me was deeply calming and centering. There is a clarity that comes in such stillness in nature. As I turned my attention to the reading I brought with me, it was like entering into conversation with each author. Portions of the texts stuck with me through the day, repeating themselves like the tunes of a familiar song.

One poem, in particular, framed the two weeks in NH, Wallace Stevens' "Credences of Summer." Stevens, like the poet of the Song of Solomon, beckons his readers to engage an unabridged fullness of life: "Let's see the very thing and nothing else/" he says, "let's see it with the hottest fire of sight/burn everything not part of it to ash/trace the gold sun about the whitened sky/*without evasion by a single metaphor*/look at it in its essential barrenness/and say this, this is the centre that I seek."

Summer for Stevens represents the pinnacle of human experience. Nothing more can be attained or learned or achieved; it is our long sought and hoped for destination, completion, fulfillment implanted in our souls; and then he says, "fix it in an eternal foliage/and fill the foliage with arrested peace…. this is the barrenness of the fertile thing that can attain no more." Sitting in silence on the porch each morning, staring out at a literal forest of summer foliage, I felt as if I understood and could communicate with the trees. Trees are the lungs of the planet; permeated and literally shaped by their years of patience and the peace patience begets. "Be still, trust, believe, partake" they encouraged me. It is not hard to imagine how those 19th century New England non-conformists became Transcendentalists at one with nature in places like New Hampshire's lake region, and even Alton Bay itself where Ralph Waldo Emerson himself once came to vacation.

Speaking of Emerson, I had with me his early journals. He was a life-long journalist; in these reflections from his teenage years at Harvard to his last year of life you can trace the development of his fertile mind; an abolitionist, an expert in religious thought, an existentialist before Nietzsche, and, with Whitman, the greatest influence on American letters. It was a line from the seventeen-year-old Emerson that came to me as Carol and I and our brother-in-law, Ron Bell, wandered off the trail one day climbing Mt. Major and found ourselves instead on a sister peak called Straightback Mountain in the Belknap range.

We'd never been on this mountain before though we'd been atop Mt. Major fifty times over the years. We'd taken a road less traveled but marked by periodic piles of stones some faithful soul had erected to indicate the way to the summit. The summit, southwest of Mt. Major, gave us, surprisingly, a view of two small lakes we'd never seen in the valley next to Winnipesaukee; and to the east a view of Winnipesaukee, Squam, Wentworth, and Ossipee plus the Presidential range fifty miles north. We stopped on the granite face of the summit among blueberry bushes and took it in without a word. Then someone uttered what we were seeing was not just the grandeur of creation but the grandeur of the Creator–glacial lakes and mountains sculpted eons ago; that's when Emerson came to mind. "Newton had a better master than the Suns and Stars," he said, "he learned of heaven ere he philosophized and after traveling through mazes of [earth and whirling planets] returned to bow his laurelled head at the feet of Jesus of Nazareth."

While we were without world news most days since the general store that sells the *New York Times* was not always on our daily round we were not without awareness of the world's woes: the mired mess of Afghanistan, the impending political conventions, the deeply polarized divide of politics and class in our nation, the wake of random gun violence that has been a tremor through the soul of the nation from Aurora, CO, in June to the Empire State Building two weeks ago to a Pathmark store in NJ this week.

These subjects surfaced inevitably in our conversations–first and foremost we thought of our younger son Douglas reporting from his post in Germany to Ranger School at Fort Benning, GA, on the very morning that his brother Ian and I rose at 4am to prepare for our half-ironman triathlon. We dedicated our event to Douglas's success at Ranger School and felt a deep bond with him–getting out of his comfort zone, anticipating his deployment to Afghanistan ten months from now. As Ian and I came down the final leg of our event he said to me, "This hurts but not nearly as much as Doug's training will. Here's to a good man!" And we did well but only wished as well as Carol in her triathlon the day before when she placed second in her age group and received a bottle of NH maple syrup.

In Wolfeboro we drove by the Romney estate with my sister and our brother in law in the boat they bought from David and Alice Gow's daughter who owns a successful business in Tilton, NH, that sells sports vehicles for every season. Romney's summer home is tasteful, large and under the watchful eye of a Coast Guard cutter anchored 100 yards off shore. Claude Welch and Jeannette Ludwig are actually Romney neighbors; fun to imagine them chatting it up on the dock.

Romney posters were everywhere in little Wolfeboro, and my hunch is Mitt will win the vote there if not elsewhere in the state where he held a Town Hall meeting in Manchester during our stay. As I say, the world and its machinations were never far away.

The unquestionable highlight of the two weeks was the chance to be with our son and daughter-in-law Julie. She has become so much a part of our lives that she is more daughter than daughter-in-law. I could go on; but her culinary skills are superlative and memories of the vacation are laced with communal feasts she prepared like the simple blueberry pancakes and turkey sausage; or basil pesto linguine with mushrooms, asparagus, red peppers and grilled chicken; or salmon with sweet potato fries and a garden salad that added ten years to my life.

Julie is the only person I can think of who doesn't bother me by making it up on a wake board on the third try, while it takes me twenty times to try before giving up. The women in our family tend to be fine athletes and who give no quarter to the men who have learned to be humble and cautious in our predictions. Spending time with our adult children is a blessing we'd always heard of and witnessed others experiencing; that experience is now enriching our lives and deepening this relatively new chapter of late middle life.

The specifics of the View from the Porch change each year, but the themes are the same: healing and renewal; immersion in the beauty of nature; clarity of perspective; and deep, loving companionship. What better than love poetry to describe this annual pilgrimage of going away with family, with my lover Carol and with our loving lover of a God.

It wasn't turtledoves we heard but two loons who'd taken up their summer residence somewhere near our end of the Bay. We could hear their haunting call and response each night and saw them on several occasions far off shore with their proud head and beak, penetrating eyes, and white breast speckled in black. "Arise, my love, my fair one and come away." Our Creator beckons us, not just our brains but our hearts, to intimate, loving relationships, to the deep bonds of shared mission and ministry, to the common vision of justice and a world at peace.

Our biggest challenge may be to let go and allow this magnificent God to love and nurture and lead us. Amen.

– Confirmation –

The Importance of Personal Experience:
A Word to The Confirmands
John 9: 24-38a

March 26, 2017

<u>Let me say a word about today</u>. You confirmands passed with flying colors through rigorous instruction from Debbie and Mark, one on one reflection and sharing with your mentors, and just this morning you successfully completed what the *Book of Order* calls 'an examination' with the elders of the church. You have written individual statements of faith, made stoles your mentors draped over your shoulders, and today you are wearing crosses that your Westminster family has given to you, which your parents have placed around you. You kneeled on these steps where generations of elders, deacons and confirmands before you have kneeled to receive the laying on of hands, the Prayer of Confirmation, and to have the Holy Spirit of God descend into your hearts as she did when you were baptized.

It's a day rich in symbolism and deep in meaning for your parents and for all of us –your church family–who have fulfilled our baptismal promise to see each of you to this moment. Your parents are remarkable. Seeing a teenager through a year of religious instruction, leading to the tender moment at which parents, for their part, are required to let go and trust, to let *you* test your heart and wings, is one of the miracles of nature without which our species, or any species, would cease to exist. The business of letting go started when you moved from a crib to a bed, a tricycle to a bicycle, when you got on the school bus the first day, and when you went away to summer camp or on an overnight field trip.

Nor does it stop or get any easier–your parents will be letting go of you for the rest of their lives–college, marriage, raising your own children. Sometimes you want them to let go, and sometimes you don't. But we know this: you wouldn't get very far in life if your parents didn't give you a nudge out of the nest. Give your parents a big hug today!

The spiritual journey you, we, all of us here are on is unique in this sense: just as a surfer can't control the wave or a sailor the wind, we can't control when and where the power and presence of God will show up in our lives. But, like

190

a surfer or sailor *we can learn to read the wind* of God's Spirit *and the power* of God's grace to guide our living. To do this, we must let go of ourselves, or that part of us that wants to control our life to avoid risk or conflict or some other version of getting out of our comfort zone.

Once you open yourself to the power of God and presence of Jesus it will demand your best, hold you accountable to yourself, cause you to grow in places you did not think you could or want to grow, and it will shape you into a person who is better than yourself. And though you are each an excellent student—do not expect to get straight A's in spirituality; there's no such thing as perfection here; but think of yourselves as beautiful works in progress. And think of us that way too because all of us are still making mistakes, still learning, growing.

<u>Let me say a word about the story of the blind man</u>—it is, hands down, a literary and spiritual jewel—with the clarity and richness of a painting by a Dutch master and the complexity and genius of a Russian novel. The writer of the Gospel of John is as brilliant as Shakespeare and wise as Solomon. I urge you to find a quiet place and read this little novella of 7 scenes and 41 verses in its entirety this afternoon. A man is born blind; the disciples ask Jesus, 'is he or are his parents sinners?' In ancient days it was thought that when someone suffered from blindness or disease God was punishing them for some sin they had committed. As I said, we all make mistakes, sometimes big mistakes. Jesus says the man is not blind because he or his parents are sinful; but his blindness will reveal the grace of God. Jesus applies mud to the man's eyes, tells him to wash, and when he does the man can see for the first time.

Confusion descends on the little village where the man lives. *Just imagine*— people who have known him all his life are not sure he is the man who was blind! The local minister and church leaders get into the act; because his healing was on a Sunday and neither the man nor the alleged healer were in church, the leaders conclude that whoever thinks they healed this man (if, in fact he is the man born blind) whoever the healer thinks he is, he is not worthy of praise but a sinner because he should have known that no one is to perform work on the Sabbath, including healing!

By now things are spiraling out of control. The minister and spiritual v.i.p.s start interrogating the man relentlessly; until the blind man suggests that perhaps what they really want to know is how to become followers of the man who healed him; the man born blind continues, 'for your information— as if I should have to remind you, the leaders of the church—were the man who healed me a sinner and not from God he could do nothing.'

191

This is the acolyte instructing the bishop. Stricken with rage, the religious leaders brand the man born blind a horrible sinner and *"drive"* away. The man is alone, Jesus reappears, informs him that indeed he is from God, and the man says, "Lord, I believe," then worships him.

<u>Let me say a word about personal experience.</u> The story of the blind man, in fact, the story of the Bible is built *on the personal experience of people who encountered God*—in a flood, a burning bush, a divided sea, in the miraculous escape from an oppressor; and later in the man Jesus—when he spoke, when he healed, and when he was raised from a tomb. *The entire biblical account is based on the personal testimony of everyday folks who experience the presence of God in their lives.* The army of Pharaoh is in hot pursuit of God's people and somehow they get through the Dead Sea and give God credit for opening the water. John's Gospel is a treasure trove of these events: water turned to wine, a lame man walks, a leper is healed, a dead man raised to life—in every instance the people say it was God.

Over and against this we have, since the advent of the scientific method, a way of validating phenomena based on physical measurement that produces what we call 'metrics' that conform to what we've discovered are laws of nature; that give us what we call 'facts.' There is much to be praised about the scientific method. Indeed, if our leaders in Washington knew better they would not cut funding to scientific research but increase funding to find more cures for disease, more ways to limit climate change, and a host of other discoveries that would ensure the health and well-being of people and the planet.

Yet faith in God, in Jesus, in the Holy Spirit is another matter altogether; it does not depend or rely upon facts; faith reduced to facts does not validate what we believe but reveals how little we actually know about the historical Jesus or God's people—Israel. If we say facts are the measure of faith and not experience or belief based on experience, we disconnect ourselves from the power of life. Faith that depends upon facts heads into the dead end of trying to confine God to a method of proof and turns faith to stone.

Did you notice in the story that the blind man affirms and clings to his story even though others try to discount it and even though he can't explain himself how or why it happened; he doesn't know who Jesus is; all he knows is that he was blind and now he sees. It is a rich irony, and true to life, that the man born blind is the only one who sees while all the others are blind. The disciples wonder if the man or his parents are sinners; the neighbors aren't sure if he really is the man born blind; the religious leaders are convinced Jesus is a sinner. Even his own parents seem unsure of their son's story and say, "ask him, he is of age."

Finally, the man born blind, realizing the people can't see him for who he is or accept his testimony, shouts, "I am the man!" And here's another irony—those who know him best—his neighbors, his minister, his own family—do not accept him or his story.

Lastly, let me say a word about how this story applies to us. The experience of Jesus spreading mud on his eyes, washing in the pool, then receiving his sight *is the blind man's connection* to the living presence of God in his life; but he doesn't know yet that it was God who opened his eyes. A great theologian once said, "we live our faith forward and understand it backward." It is more important to live our faith than to understand it. The blind man doesn't understand what has happened to him until he talks with Jesus. All he knows is that he was blind and now he sees. But this is the foundation for what becomes his faith.

You might say that all of us are blind like the people in the story. We wake up every day and go about the routine of school, work, play—not thinking of Jesus or God or anything other than getting through the next exam or business project or sports competition. Then something happens, some old obstacle is removed, some wound suddenly healed, some paralyzing fear taken away. And we realize we've been given a gift. We live in a society that will insist on all kinds of rational explanations for the miracles that occur in our lives and reject any explanations having to do with faith or God.

I say that this journey of faith is like a surfer catching a wave or a sailor catching the wind to propel the boat. We don't control the wind or the wave, or the power that gives us life and that heals us and performs miracles. What we can do is learn to read the water and when a wave appears paddle our boards into its crest and let it take us further than we ever imagined possible. We can learn to watch the weather, the clouds, the ripples on the surface of the lake, the condition of the sails and when a gust descends position the boat to let its invisible power propel us to our greatest dreams and God's destination.

You each had to reach into some personal experience of God to write your statements of faith; some voice, some memory caused you to choose the words and write those wonderful statements about God. That's the first step— to listen to your life; to be still and let the voice of God speak through the news of the day, through a friend, or a cry for help, or a call for justice. Then pray, and pray some more; talk with your mentors, talk with your family; and what will happen is that Jesus will appear in those cries or calls or conversations.

Some people say faith is caught, not taught. If faith were merely about facts it would be easy to teach. But it's not; faith is about being let go and learning to use your own wings, it's about letting yourself go and getting out of your comfort zone, it's about keeping watch for God every day for that big roller on the horizon, and then getting you and your board ready for the thrill of your life.

I'm not talking about standing on a long board in the tunnel of a 30-foot Laguna Beach roller, I'm talking about something better than that; about using your gifts to make the world—your school, your neighborhood, your college someday—more just, more kind, more open than when you found it. There are many metaphors for the abundant life you embraced today when you reconfirmed your baptismal vows: riding a big wave, having a sea part to let you pass when you thought you were trapped, having your eyes opened to a new world, being raised from the depth of despair, from death itself.

Jesus told the man to wash the mud from his eyes in the pool of Siloam which means 'sent.' The word 'apostle' is taken from the Greek word that means 'one sent.' That's what your confirmation is about, being sent into the world to use your wings, to be a brave work in progress for Jesus's sake. Don't be afraid of making mistakes; Jesus will give you your life back again and again. Amen.

– World Communion –

A Church for All Species
Hebrews 2: 5-12

October 4, 2015

It's World Communion—when Christians of all kinds around the earth celebrate the central sacrament of our faith—a sacrament about which, even while we celebrate it, we still find ourselves in conflict over a five-hundred-year-old argument. There is a certain irony of the church celebrating its central liturgical rite together but in disagreement. This "Sunday in common for communion" started in 1933 at Shadyside Presbyterian Church in Pittsburgh, PA and grew out of an ecumenical movement that sought to promote Christian unity.

But now, almost a century after that first World Communion Sunday we might wonder if there will ever come a day when Christians will be one in Christ–rather than fragmented by internal and external, deal-breaking disputes, like the church's ongoing battle with the culture. Richard Stearns, president of World Vision, an evangelical mission agency, says, "I have been deeply grieved by the damage done to the reputation of Christianity in recent years by Christians shaking their fists at the culture. Perhaps the shortest definition of God in Scripture," he says, "is 1John 4:8, 'God is love.' We should focus on showing the world the simplicity of that revolutionary idea."[i]

What would it take to quell religious strife within the church and between those in the church who harangue the culture with fundamentalist fist-shaking? How to get warring parties to lay down their arms and reaffirm that we are called above all else, by both Testaments and Jesus himself to "love God with our whole mind, heart, soul and strength and our neighbor as ourselves"?

Perhaps the biggest message of the Pope's recent visit is that we don't need to wait for a meeting of the cardinals or an international congress of religions to approve any edict or statement; rather we can and should proceed, right now, right where we are to demonstrate the gospel's radical call to love. Which is what Jesus did. At a time when the religious authorities of his day made a mockery of biblical justice and ethics, Jesus went about his ministry fulfilling the spirit of the law. "I come not to change but to fulfill the law and prophets," he said.

Perhaps churches and church leaders doing what they felt the bible and their conscience called them to do would be a recipe for ecclesiastical anarchy; but could that be any worse than the present state of affairs? Diverse coalitions might gather around visionary leaders and ideas like Pope Francis and climate change or Bishop Tutu and restorative justice or Brian McLaren's finding common ground in mission beyond the culture wars. The Pope's call for such a church has appeal beyond Roman Catholicism. "I prefer a church which is bruised, hurting and dirty," he said, "because it has been out on the streets rather than a church which is unhealthy from being confined." World Communion could be a call not just for one church but one human family, sustaining one world.

What would such a church look like? What would its priorities be? Some church leaders, Francis among them, are connecting compassion with climate change; calling the nations to take impending environmental disaster seriously. Here's a simple analogy. We have some leaky roofs here at Westminster. You'll be hearing more about them as the session is in the early stages of organizing a capital and mission campaign. But because the roof is leaking, everything else inside is at risk: our landmark Aeolian Skinner Organs, our Steinway pianos, our beautifully restored sanctuary, our refinished wooden floors, our pews, our business office and technology. There has already been some damage. Yes, there are other capital issues that need to be fixed, but the roof is the top priority.

Like Westminster's roof, there are holes in the roof of the world--the ozone layer--that protects earth from the relentless heat and infra-red rays of the sun. The holes are caused by carbon-generated gases--from combustion engines in cars, coal-burning power plants, and a long list of items we still use and are not willing to give up.

As the earth heats--even with the reduction in emissions called for at the UN summit in Paris in November--the increase in warming will still be six degrees by 2030. That doesn't sound like much, but six degrees globally will result in more melting of the polar ice caps resulting in higher levels for the oceans resulting in the disappearance of low lying lands--like New York City, New Orleans, San Francisco, Miami, you can take your pick of coastal cities.

The developed nations will figure out drastic and monumentally expensive ways to retrench, but for underdeveloped nations, people will be displaced and unable to find work and food and shelter. These shortages will plague the human family. Not to mention that thousands of plant and animal species could become extinct, starting with the polar bears unable to sustain themselves without their glacial habitat.

There was a glimpse of what, at first, seemed like an increment of good news from India last week when India's leaders announced they would strive for the emission standards called for at the summit in December. However, they said, we cannot provide a date when we will meet those standards. Why? Because India is still developing its economy through a vast infrastructure of coal-fired industries. When pressed on the date they responded with a good question: Why should India or any nation like it be asked to foot the bill the developed nations ran up by growing their economies and industries with cheap coal?

I can imagine that it would take something similar to the arms agreements we made with Saudi Arabia and Israel to get the Iran nuclear deal to work. We are providing vast armaments to those nations who feel at risk with Iran. If you want us to reduce our emissions, India might say, then pay for the difference it will cost us to convert from coal to safer fuels and technologies. Try to get that proposal through a Congress in which some representatives still doubt that climate change is real! Or what kind of corporate leader or stockholders would it take to redistribute wealth by restructuring earnings and profits to convert developing nations to climate-safe technology? It would require an all-encompassing multi-national, public/private partnership similar to the one formed during WWII.

Just as we have other things to fix in this building—heating and plumbing, stained glass windows, oak doors, flooring—there are serious matters in our nation and world that cry out for attention: race relations, rights for women, gays and lesbians, income inequality, educational opportunity, health care for the poorest, gun control—all of which are of major importance and need to be addressed to get our house and world in order. But if we don't fix the roof of this church it won't matter what we do with the windows or wiring systems; just as if we don't fix the atmosphere, human and economic justice will be moot.

I am not proposing that we focus on climate change to the exclusion of all the other matters that the church is called to address. But I am suggesting that climate change needs to be close to if not at the very top of our personal and church agenda. It would mean educating ourselves, changing daily living habits, fighting a fight that isn't as visible as the scourge of poverty or lack of gun control.

On this World Communion Sunday, we need to re-arrange our theological and social justice priorities. Rather than allow Calvin's or Rome's definitions of communion to continue to divide us, perhaps we all need to recommit to the greatest commandment—to love God and neighbor. In fact, that ancient, simple admonition seems more important to a world threatened with climate change than all the wars that took place over the meaning of communion that still divide us.

If love of God and neighbor eclipsed our liberal and conservative political agendas, somehow transcended our economic self-interest and surpassed our theological disputes, we might find our hearts and minds opened to new possibilities for a safer, sustainable world. They say the rats are poised to inherit the earth; that after we destroy human civilization including much of plant and animal life by burning up the planet, those repugnant rodents will take over. Apparently, rats can adapt and reproduce so rapidly that a transformed landscape and vastly reduced food sources will pose little obstacle to them.

But then while rats are smart and adaptive (and remember they are, nevertheless, God's creatures just trying to survive) humans are endowed with God-given gifts like ingenuity and cooperation—*"You have made them a little lower than God and crowned them with glory and honor. You have given them dominion over the works of your hands; you have put all things under their feet, all sheep and oxen, the beasts of the field, the birds of the air, the fish of the sea."* Isn't it time we start living like God's people! May this simple meal today, rather than a worn-out argument that divides us, be a rallying cry to become the caretakers of the earth God has already equipped us to be. Amen.

i. Nicholas Kristof, "A Pope for All Species," *The New York Times*, September 9, 2015, A35.

– Reformation Sunday –

Faith Works: The Bottom Line for Presbyterians
Matthew 22: 34-46

October 29, 2017

Five hundred years and twelve days ago Martin Luther nailed his 95 theses to the chapel door in Wittenberg, Germany. That act of inviting public debate over the core values of the church was like holding a match to the dead structures of the medieval world. The result was the leveling of the landscape of western civilization in a social and political conflagration the likes of which we have not seen since.

Luther's Faith alone, Scripture alone, God alone and Priesthood of All Believers were the points on a theological compass that guided the infant Protestant church then and still guides the church today. Once the Protestant genie was out of the bottle communities as like the Roman Church as Lutherans and Anglicans and as different as Presbyterians and Baptists began forming. No longer did geography determine what parish one belonged to, but theology became the determining factor for church affiliation.

It feels like we are on the verge of another great upheaval of church and society. Five hundred years is a long time for any structure to remain viable. As in the medieval world, many institutions now are operating with outdated models. In the 16th century the printing press, emerging capitalism, and population shifts from rural to urban centers were the drivers of change. Similar forces are at work today. Yet, the one constant is the longing, call it spiritual hunger, for a fulfilled and satisfying life. One of the biggest barriers to spiritual renewal in the early 1500s, and in any age, is the church itself. When the church gets distracted with internal issues from administration to governance to funding it can lose touch with its primary mission and priorities and cease to be relevant. There are stress fractures now in virtually every national denomination, not to mention systems of education, health care, and business and commercial enterprises. It's as if an old world is disappearing.

I attended a luncheon last week before the Auburn Seminary board meeting to discuss Auburn's relationship to the Presbyterian Church (USA). The conversation ranged from questioning whether there should be any connection to the denomination to the conviction that Auburn has a moral obligation to the PCUSA. The discussion would have been inconceivable ten years ago. Auburn president Katharine Henderson said there is not one of the denomination's theological institutions that is not debating its mission and Presbyterian identity.

'What is it that is essential to being Presbyterian?' we asked ourselves. And what kept coming back as answers were a handful of core values, principles that determine what is important, how to live and who God is. Presbyterians have always recognized that each of us may have a different take on the essential tenets of our faith, yet we do so within the larger frame of the monotheistic God of the Bible, religious freedom and a democratic form of government. It is freedom of conscience vs. dogmatism that keeps the church grounded yet flexible.

Today's text is another crucible moment in the history of the people of God. Jesus' response to the final attempt by his critics to entrap him by the formative confrontation, before his arrest, between not the old religion so much as the old religious structures and what would emerge as the Christian faith. The question, 'which is the greatest law' of all the over 600 laws of the Torah was designed to by impossible to answer, as the Pharisees would inevitably raise the importance of some other law Jesus failed to mention. Yet, when he identified love of God with all strength, heart and mind and a second commandment as great as the first—to love neighbor as self—it was an answer based on the Torah that was impossible for the Pharisees to refute and thus silenced them. Jesus' question to them that they cannot answer clearly establishes his superiority over his interrogators and leads to the authorities' decision to eliminate Jesus.

It would be hard to find any text more central to 'faith works' and the Reformation than Matthew's suspenseful account of Jesus articulating the core principle of our faith in a showdown with the forces of darkness. What gives Jesus' answer its weight is that the love he refers to is not a state of emotion but an act of the will; the word for love here is "agape"; the kind of love exhibited in God's covenants with Israel.

Even more critical to note is that Matthew equates the neighbor whom Jesus says we are to love not only with the fellow Israelite but the enemy whom Jesus says in the Sermon on the Mount we are to embrace. And finally, the combination of neighbor love with love of God makes these two commandments inseparable. To love God is to love one's neighbor and to love one's neighbor is to love God.

Whatever else it may mean to be a Presbyterian, this is the essence of who we are and why we are here–to love God and neighbor and not just my neighbor my friend but my neighbor my adversary and nemesis. While this appears to be just an aspiration, —a goal—it is nevertheless a goal well within reach because we are each made in the image of God.

But there's one more piece to this commandment: it is hard to love God and my neighbors in the developing world if I am polluting the planet and using a disproportionate proportion of earth's resources. It is hard to love God and my neighbor if the life style I enjoy is made possible by supporting businesses and industries that harm others. At the Auburn board meeting we heard a presentation from three Goldman Sachs employees about socially sustainable investing for Auburn's endowment; this form of investing is expected to leap into the trillions of dollars over the next few years. People may disagree about what to invest in, but what I hear Jesus talking about and what I heard Bob Bojdak talking about this morning is that faith works when we accept the spiritual imperative and moral obligation to make the world better in our daily sphere of life.

The marvelous thing is Bob learned that understanding of Christian commitment from his parents to be sure but later, as a young adult, from the Jesuits and not the Presbyterians; yet, he found a Presbyterian church home in which to live out that truth for himself and his family.

Maybe what the Reformation was good for was not creating a plethora of new churches but for cutting through the distraction and deception of self-serving religion and outdated, oppressive power structures and then identifying amidst the competing voices of culture the one voice, the one truth that leads to a fulfilled life.

That's why we're here, unless I miss my guess. Yes, it's for the music, yes, it's for thought provoking sermons and education and mission–but at the end of the day we are here to belong to and participate with a community of people committed to a great commandment that makes them and the world better.

In three weeks we'll be asked to make our financial pledge to Westminster for 2018. There are lots of places we can devote our discretionary dollars. Schools need libraries and labs; museums need new wings to house great art; hospitals need the latest technology for battling disease. But in these broken and cynical times, there are few things as important as building bridges of healing and peace that the love Jesus is talking about today makes possible.

If the name "Presbyterian" fades from history it won't be the end of the world, but if that love so radical, so divine isn't embodied in people like you and me and in communities like this one it could very well be the end of the world. I don't recall times when the choice for where and how to 'make the world better' was ever so clear and compelling as it is now, in 2017. Amen.

– Stewardship –

Earn This*
Hebrews 12:1-3

October 28, 2012

Just a week ago our family was at Fort Benning, Georgia, for our younger son's graduation from Ranger School. One thing I've noticed since Doug has been in the military is how the Army, like many organizations, perpetuates itself and its mission by remembering its past—in uniform pins, ribbons, troop banners, halls of history; and stories. Like the speeches we heard at the ceremony about historic Ranger missions demonstrating extraordinary valor.

These stories were inspiring enough, but then the keynote speaker recounted the bravery displayed by one Ranger in one late 20th century conflict in Africa where US forces were serving a peace-keeping role. The story of this soldier's calm amidst battle, risking his life to save the lives of others, and ultimately sacrificing his own life was a wakeup call for all of us. What is it that inspires people to reach for their best, to put their very lives on the line, to exceed what they or anyone else thought possible? The Rangers have figured out it's knowing who you are which begins by remembering your ancestors and their stories.

And this is what today's reading does for the church. Hebrews remembers the heroes of faith. The chapter preceding today's reading retells their accomplishments from Abraham and Sarah, to Isaac and Jacob, to Joseph and Moses. To a long list of minor figures who each played their part in God's history. So the writer says today, "Therefore, since we are surrounded by such a great cloud of witnesses, let us run with perseverance the race set before us." In other words, let us adopt and embrace the same values and vision—the faith—that guided them. What motivates and keeps an Army or church strong are stories of valor of those who served it.

What I'd like to suggest today, Dedication Sunday, is that Westminster Presbyterian Church has a noble, brave history right here in this city and region; and what we are doing committing ourselves to support this ministry for the year to come is nothing less than aligning ourselves with the bold action, far reaching mission and stand for justice our ancestors in this church took before us.

You could go back to the founders who built this 900-seat sanctuary with a congregation of only forty members. Or, the Reverend Dr. Samuel van Vranken Holmes, two generations later, standing with a dozen other pastors and the mayor of Buffalo on an East Side street. The mayor asked the clergy if their churches would help meet the needs of what were then thousands of poor, young German immigrants. The other clergy responded, "Don't call us, we'll call you," but Dr. Holmes turned to the mayor and said "we'll take all the blocks from here to there" as he pointed out a huge swath of homes. He could do that because he knew the people of this congregation would respond. He knew that they knew that it was not only the right thing to do but what folks used to call the Christian thing to do. Not long afterward, Westminster House was built and Miss Holmes, no relation to him, was hired as director. It was the second settlement house in America.

No doubt you have your favorite stories. In each generation, there have been defining moments when the clergy and people of this church have stepped up and stepped forward regardless of what other churches were doing or not doing; stepped up and stepped into situations when some injustice needed to be addressed or some suffering alleviated.

I'm thinking of Dr. Butzer, up late, bent over his desk, writing the letters, hundreds of letters to Westminster and Buffalo boys on the front lines of WWII; letters that some of their families still possess. Or the Sunday night in 1950 when Dr. Butzer rushed to the scene of the fire engulfing nearby Temple Beth Zion, embraced Rabbi Fink and arm in arm watched the blaze destroy the old Temple. Standing before that fire, Dr. Butzer turned to Rabbi Fink and said, "Our church is your synagogue until you build a new home." For over a year, members of Temple Beth Zion greeted one another for Shabbat Friday evenings in this sanctuary.

Dr. Ray Kiely, Al Butzer's successor, and this congregation in the 1960s stepped into the burning controversy of red-lining here in the city; when realtors systematically blocked the purchase of homes by people of color in specific, all-white neighborhoods. Dr. Kiely opposed such bald racism and said so publicly and often, and members of this church stood by him.

The following decade when a young candidate for ministry on Long Island was told he could not be ordained because he was gay, a forty-year struggle for that right began in the Presbyterian church. It took its toll on the denomination and this congregation. But the Rev. Tom Stewart and core members here took up the fight for gay and lesbian ordination. When More Light Presbyterians was founded in the late 70s Westminster became one of its first member-congregations; and when our Session said our doors were open to gays and lesbians as full and participating members of this church we were formally charged by six local congregations for violating the constitution of the church. An ecclesiastical court case went all the way to the Permanent Judicial Commission of the national church which exonerated us. But the work of education and consciousness-raising had just begun, so our elders went, in small groups, to dozens of churches to explain our position. And one year ago, October 5, we conducted what we believe was the first gay wedding in a Presbyterian church in the State of New York.

In the 1980s when demonstrators were intimidating women visiting their physicians at a Planned Parenthood clinic, members of this church and others helped form a safe corridor. And two days after 9/11 this room was filled with grieving Western New Yorkers who stood side by side in solidarity with American Muslims. A year later the BPO played here on the first anniversary of that tragic moment in American history. In 1998 when Dr. Barnett Slepian, a doctor in support of women's choice, was killed standing at his kitchen window by a sniper's bullet, the community of Western New York gathered once again in this sanctuary to mourn and to call for justice. Westminster's mission dollars and volunteers have helped establish everything from senior housing at St. John the Baptist Church to Benedict House for AIDS victims to Vive La Casa—a shelter for political refugees from around the world.

The values and valor of those generations are in the spiritual DNA of this congregation and shape our ministry today. The settlement house tradition continues in our Westminster Economic Development Initiative on the West Side with new immigrant families: a jobs, housing, education program that gives children and families a foothold of hope and the chance to make their own way.

The work of interfaith understanding and cooperation has expanded since TBZ used this sanctuary to worship; it includes ground-breaking programs with Muslims and Jews like Mitzvah Day, Abraham's Walk and our annual Understanding Islam education series; and did you know that a Zen Buddhist meditation community has met here weekly for over a decade?

The stand for civil rights, justice and compassion fuels new programs like Re-entry Friends that helps recent prison parolees back into productive living in a world that regards them with deep suspicion and distrust.

You'd have to search long and hard to find a mainline church or any church that embraces such diversity and supports causes and programs like these combined with worship in one of Western New York's finest sanctuaries, accompanied by Western New York's finest church choir and music ministry.

205

That's a combination that simply does not exist anywhere else in our community.

The reason the Army tells those Ranger stories is because people forget. It is easy to focus on ordinary routine and maintenance; it's easy to worry about the daily drudgery of life in the Army (or civilian life) and forget the glory; forget that you are part of an organization that has helped change the world.

How easily it could all disappear. We're not fighting Sunday morning sports or busy lives that leave no time to volunteer; those are symptoms of a larger foe: the fragmentation of human relationships; the search for purpose through consuming and acquiring; the struggle to secure our place and our children's place in the American caste system; and, of course, the same kind of bigotry and bias that plagues every generation.

What we are doing today committing to another year of support is more than determining a sum of money; we are reclaiming the proud heritage of this congregation which cannot be maintained by any amount of dollars alone; in fact, it can only be secured by your dedication and my dedication to be better than ourselves; to continue to see to it that the name of this church is associated with hope and help; with excellence in worship; with care for all ages, especially the spiritual nurture of our children.

What we are committing to today is more than money. It is to the health and vitality of a church without which Buffalo would be poorer, colder, and more desperate. Yesterday, at the memorial service for a church member who sang in our choir and retired with her husband to the south years ago, the husband asked how we are doing at Westminster; I told him about the programs I just mentioned to you and he said, "Then the challenge is being met." But I wasn't comfortable agreeing with him. I wasn't comfortable saying everything was fine thank you very much because we are always only one generation away from extinction. And you and I are that generation. All the brave and faithful people who preceded us and delivered this treasured church into our care are now gone. And the future we have depends upon our resolve, with God's help, to live as big and brave and generously as they did.

Maybe you remember the 1998 Steven Spielberg film titled "Saving Private Ryan." The story depicts a US Army Ranger Captain John H. Miller played by Tom Hanks who led his squad through the Normandy Invasion at Omaha Beach, behind enemy lines, to find and bring home Private First-Class James Francis Ryan played by Matt Damon. The film is based on the true story of the Niland brothers from North Tonawanda, NY, three of whom were killed in WWII and the youngest of whom was saved by a squad of Rangers who gave their lives for him because the Joint Chiefs General George C. Marshall wanted to prevent those parents from losing all their sons to war.

In the film, shortly after Captain Miller and his squad find Private Ryan in a small French village, a German armored division storms the town which Miller and his Rangers single-handedly defend until air and tank support arrive to win the day and ensure Private Ryan's return to the United States. The story ends with Captain Miller, mortally wounded and most of his squad killed, holding a bridge German tanks were attempting to cross; and as the first Allied planes start flying overhead Miller looks up at Private Ryan and says with his last breath, "Earn this."

We're not facing enemy tanks these days, but we are dealing with a struggling economy and city with enough hurt and suffering to keep lots of Westminsters busy. As I think about the writer of Hebrews and those generations and leaders of Westminster through the past century, as I think about the Jesus stories Mark has been telling these past weeks that 'you need to lose your life to find it,' I can hear all of them saying to us, "Earn this."

We can do as little or as much as we want to validate their sacrifice, to justify their efforts to ensure that we would have a church. But anything less than they gave will be too little.

What will it take to maintain Westminster's ministry? It will take making our life together your highest giving priority. It's why Dr. Holmes designed this arch of the martyrs—to remind us every time we sit in these pews of the extraordinary valor with which those first followers of Jesus gave their lives.

That's how much it will take. That's what it will cost you and me. Are you surprised? I didn't think so. Do we have it in us? There's no question in my mind that we do. It just means committing, this morning, to life and service we would be willing to die for. Gianna, whom we just baptized, and her friends are counting on us. Amen.

* The title of this sermon was borrowed from a John Buchanan sermon

– Ordination Sunday –

Called
1 Samuel 3:1-10; John 1:43-51

January 11, 2015

In the bible, humans often try to put God in some small, manageable box; we enforce the letter, not the spirit of the law and wrap ourselves in pious, public ritual. But God is forever trying to humanize us, make us real by not staying confined to our narrow definitions and small expectations for the holy. The result is God is often not where we expect to find him and often in the last place we'd choose to look.

That's the theme today. The boy Samuel, valet for the old priest Eli, ends up being the one God calls–not the seasoned, wise, faithful clergyman; and the story from John features skeptical, naysayer Nathaniel as the one Jesus picks to be his new disciple. Then there's Jesus himself–a no-account carpenter from a no-where town who turns out to be the very savior of the human race. All of this tends to up-end our notion of how things ought to work–the one with seniority or the white, educated, middle class male, or the one with academic titles and honors, or the one who has financial pull and political power ought to get the favored, revered position.

Yet, the bible sends the clear message again and again that this is not how God works. Starting with Abraham and Sarah, a young, naïve couple, all the way through to St. Paul–a persecutor of God's people. Moses, Jacob, Ruth, Rachel, the prophets everyone, David the boy who would be king, the disciples of course–rarely was ever a group of such misfits assembled for any purpose let alone to launch a movement that would outsmart and outlast the greatest empire on earth. So if you are here today, trying to remain anonymous, unnoticed, or stay below the radar and then quietly go home to your familiar routine, you may be just the candidate God is looking for to lead a revival or change a life.

Rarely does any reason or excuse not to be selected or called get in the way. Abram and Sarai were just kids when the future of humanity was placed in their laps. Sarah was old and barren when she was told she would become matriarch of a great nation. Moses had a bad stutter but was the one God pegged as lead negotiator with Pharaoh. David was a shepherd boy who played the tin whistle when he was called to fight–winner take all–mountain man Goliath. Waffle-man Peter, the solid-as-a-rock foundation of the church? Really? Mistress of the night Mary Magdalene invited to the inner circle of Jesus friends. What was he thinking!

Raise up the lowly, topple the mighty. That's how God works, and he seems to take pleasure and delight in doing so. These are good readings for this day in particular because we are ordaining and installing four new deacons and two new elders. I am not suggesting that we have looked in the down and out places to find these wonderful people to serve the church. In fact, we have a very careful selection process to make sure we have the best candidates possible.

What I am saying is when it comes to the church, when it comes to making this place run the way it's supposed to, when it comes to tackling the most important things God wants us to tackle—we are wise to remember that God works in ways the world considers foolish; God brings about results with unexpected and unorthodox representatives and agents; and God is not above using procedures the Harvard Business School or Good Housekeeping Approval Committee would frown upon.

And therein is our liberation. If we don't have to have an MBA or be among the philanthropic class or have achieved some award-winning recognition in order to have the Holy Spirit select us and work through us, then we can stop thinking that the nominating committee or chairperson of the taskforce should find someone else. Instead of assuming we need to know more about the bible or have better church attendance or wield some position of authority around here, we can trust that God has already given us what we need to be called to some important ministry. The barriers have been removed. We might be called at any minute to do any of the things Jesus did: heal the sick, feed the hungry, visit those in some prison of loneliness. In fact, we are surrounded by real, human need right in this congregation before we even set foot in the world.

Bill Blakeslee, a former stalwart member of our choir but officially and enthusiastically a member of Trinity Episcopal Church, son of an Episcopal priest, liked to make the distinction between Christianity and what he called "Churchianity." Christianity is the practice of Christ-like principles in day-to-day living; Churchianity is a life that makes everything religious, deified, holier than thou, but ends up being of little use or relevance to the world. Churchianity thinks that to be Christian we need to be squeaky clean and morally perfect; Churchianity in practice looks a lot like the Pharisees who prayed aloud in public places and wore sack-cloth and ashes on holy days, but when the world wasn't looking kicked the dog and cheated on their taxes.

209

What I am saying today is that when all is said and done what matters is whether our hearts are in it or not; whether we are willing to admit that we're bored to tears with the practice of a religion that is hollow and empty. Rather, let us ask if we are willing to consider taking a risk turning our lives over to an unpredictable higher power; a God who has the best interests of humanity at heart, especially those overlooked by our limited justice and relief for those who suffer.

What God wants to make of us is the *real* you and the *real* me—not the puffed-up versions, or the Facebook-everything-in-my-life-is-fun version—but the version that bears even a small longing to have impact and bring hope. We don't need more committees, we need more people willing to take the plunge into the future of a ministry that might not exist yet, or one that does but needs willing hands and hearts. I am talking about more than the pursuit of happiness. I am talking about the experience of satisfaction, connection, and being part of something bigger than ourselves that may not be finished in our lifetime but will be our deepest joy when we close your eyes at night and then on that day yet to come for the last time on this earth.

I am talking about what David Brooks referred to as a "meaningful life" in a column this past week: "Happiness is about enjoying the present; meaning is about dedicating oneself to the future. Happiness is about receiving; meaningfulness is about giving. Happiness is about upbeat moods and nice experiences. People leading meaningful lives experience a deeper sense of satisfaction."

You see while we are installing new elders and deacons today who surely need your prayers and support, this ministry, this church, their leadership won't get to where we need to go unless they can count on you and me being willing to go "all in" with them. Sure, some of us are here to heal or reflect or take a time out from some difficult experience; and some of us are here faithfully because being in church and worshipping God make us feel better as the week begins. And that's fine.

But what I am saying today as we witness God call a mere shepherd boy to become a great leader of Israel and Jesus call a prickly, skeptic sourpuss to become a person of compassion and service and as we ordain and install women and men out of our midst who are putting themselves on the line today, what I am saying is that there is a greater calling for *all of us*, beyond our comfort zones of routine. When we look at the people God calls and uses in the bible not only are we left with no excuses to respond in some way to the plethora of needs around us, but we ought to take heart. If God can change the world with a pimply boy or woman of ill repute or fundamentalist and persecutor, imagine what God can do with us!

So the assignment today is to listen. God is calling; you may hear that call for the first time and think it's for someone else, you may hear it a second time and conclude you're the wrong person, but if the voice persists even in a whisper–it's you God, and this church is waiting for to say 'Yes." Amen.

CPSIA information can be obtained
at www.ICGtesting.com
Printed in the USA
FSHW02n0834290818
51667FS